ENDORSEMENTS:

"I don't know anyone who hasn't been touched by a friend or loved one's experience with Alzheimer's disease. This book is a journey of one my church members: a daughter who relied upon her relationship with Jesus to care for her parents, being an instrument of the grace her Savior extended to her. In Chapter 5, Knapp asks: "Do you believe that God can be trusted with the details of whatever you're facing?" This book is filled with Scriptures, prayers and personal experiences that reveal God can be trusted to accompany us through life's storms. The book will benefit those in need of encouragement, tips for caregiving or simply the courage to face their personal fears and failures. While Knapp offers an incredible gift to reflect upon and integrate her unique experiences in caring for her mother, the power for God's glory revealed in her personal life, biblical life and prayers is evident. May God use this book to encourage us all to trust Him in all things and experience the blessings that await!"

Tad Rogers
Pastor, First Baptist Church, Mountain Home, Arkansas

"Beautiful, vulnerable, encouraging in its insight and authenticity. Cheryl Crofoot Knapp has a gift for coming alongside caregivers and lifting up their tired arms. Filled with hard-won wisdom and abounding grace."

New York Times Bestselling author, Tosca Lee

Undefeated Innocence

How God Helped My Parents and Me
Navigate the Alzheimer's Journey

Cheryl Crofoot Knapp

Founder, Regifted Grace® Ministry

WESTBOW
PRESS®
A DIVISION OF THOMAS NELSON
& ZONDERVAN

Editorial Credits:
Katy Gray, Senior Editor, klgray413@gmail.com.
Rebecca Cooper.

Photography Credits:
Paula Preston, Photographer, www.paulapreston.com.
Picture Place—Barry Howell, Photographer.

WestBow Press books may be ordered through booksellers or by contacting:

WestBow Press
A Division of Thomas Nelson & Zondervan
1663 Liberty Drive
Bloomington, IN 47403
www.westbowpress.com
1 (866) 928-1240

ISBN: 978-1-5127-7898-4 (sc)
ISBN: 978-1-5127-7899-1 (hc)
ISBN: 978-1-5127-7897-7 (e)

Library of Congress Control Number: 2017903622

Print information available on the last page.

WestBow Press rev. date: 03/24/2017

For my beloved mama—Beverly (age 3).

Dedications

Father
Donovan Richard Crofoot
September 28, 1928—August 4, 2010

Mother
Beverly Harriet Harms Crofoot
June 25, 1934—June 30, 2016

Cousin
Curtis Calvine Crofoot
November 8, 1937—January 3, 2017

The millions of lives lost to Alzheimer's Disease,
the 47,000,000 people around the world with dementia,
and the sacrificial caregivers who love them.

Acknowledgments

Caregiving taught me a lot about gains and losses. It taught me about discovering courage within myself and the importance of having the love and support from those around me. As the dust continues to settle and I set the plumb line to a new normal, I want to acknowledge a few of the special people in my life who shared their yokes with me to help shoulder the Alzheimer's journey.

Abba Father, thank you for giving me this story to tell, showering me with your grace and mercy, and carrying me when the struggles knocked me down.

Mom and Dad, thank you for inspiring me when I was young, teaching me about life, and showing me the road to independence. You continued to inspire me as your years of walking alongside me were coming to a close. You held my hand when I was young, and I held your hands when you grew old. I love you always and am so grateful that our Abba Father chose you to be my parents.

Chuck, thank you for sharing your unconditional and fearless love in abundance with me, adopting my parents as your own, and sacrificing so much. I love you always and am so grateful to be your wife.

Tom and Matt, the joy and richness you bring into my life is indescribable. You gave me the gift of understanding how deep a mother's love can run. I love you and am so very proud of you.

Lori, you are the sister I always dreamed of having. Thank you for your forgiving love and inspiring courage. We have many laughs, tears, and stories left to share. Adel, thank you for loving Mom as your own. Allison and Ashley, the love for your grandparents was undeniably radiant. They were blessed to call you granddaughters. I love you all like crazy.

Thank you to those I call *family*, regardless of whether or not we are related by blood. You have unselfishly loved, supported, and sacrificed. You understood when you didn't get to see us very often. I love you.

Karen and Kristen, thank you for being my besties, my forever best friends, who always understood even without words, never judged, always loved, and led me closer to Jesus. We have shared plenty of laughter and tears through our adventures together. I love you both. Here's to Lucy and Ethel, and to Thelma and Louise.

Thank you to those I call *friend*. You have prayed for me, encouraged me, made me laugh, and taught me how to be a better friend through your compassionate devotion in our friendships. Thank you for not only asking how Mom was doing, but for also asking how I was doing. I love you.

Katy Gray, my friend first and awesome editor second, I couldn't have gotten to the finish line without you. Thank you for understanding God's vision for *Undefeated Innocence* and relentlessly encouraging me and straightening out my grammar. I love you.

Pastor Tad, thank you for being God's vessel to teach me through your encouragement and sermons how God never fails. He always takes us where we need to go, pushes us when we need prodding, and holds us up in the dark hours. Thank you for calling and praying while we were still in the emergency room after I said goodbye to my mama. We love you.

Pastor Kevin and Nicole, words aren't possible to thank you for uprooting your schedule to race to the hospital and wipe my tears away. Thank you for your prayers in this journey and for being my *beautiful* prayer warriors, hand holders, and cheerleaders. Thank you for believing in telling this story. We love you.

Tosca Lee, we're in the business of putting words together, but words aren't adequate to express how your faith, friendship, commitment, mentoring, and encouragement have meant to me. Even as you faced your own deadlines, you gave me the priceless gift of your time to guide my way. Thank you so much. I love you.

None of this was possible without my team of prayer warriors and the reviewers who took the time to read two hundred pages in a weekend. Chad Allen, God sent you to provide me with your expertise, challenges, books, and formidable coaching. My self-doubts were erased and you dared me to succeed. Boom! Rebecca Cooper, thank you for polishing and bringing this story to the finish line on such short notice and for braving the end notes. I love you guys.

Randall and Lori Drake, and your gracious staff at Drake Law Firm, thank you for walking our family through every aspect of elder care and probate. You held our hands, wiped away our tears, and offered to us the wisdom and friendship we needed to be caregivers for both Mom and Dad. Thank you for making us a part of your family. We love you.

Our family is grateful for the angels on earth who provided love and nursing care to Mom and Dad at Hillcrest Nursing Home, Good Samaritan Village of Mountain Home, and Gassville Therapy and Living. We particularly need to thank the nurses and staff from the sixth floor at Baxter Regional Medical Center. We know you loved our mom, too. Annette, thank you for being our advocate. Your compassion for Mom and me during her final twenty-four hours still brings me to tears. Thank you for holding me in the emergency room and for always understanding how it felt. You are one of a kind. We love you.

I always thank my God for you because of
his grace given you in Christ Jesus.

(1 Corinthians 1:4)

Contents

Preface

Others said, "You are blessed." I was broken.
Others said, "You are strong." I was scared.
Others said, "You are courageous." I was cowardly.
Others said, "You are brave." I was barely standing.
Others said, "You lost much." I loved much.
Others said, "You gave much." I received grace.

We hold newborn babies and believe we look into eyes of innocence—lives undefeated by mortal existence. Children grow; life gets complicated. Innocence erodes. We hold someone with Alzheimer's and believe we look into eyes of fear. Lifetime memories fade like shadows, a decade at a time. Lives are lived in reverse. Alzheimer's attacks its innocent victims. But it doesn't defeat innocence. Those who have it seemingly return to being a young child and regain simplicity. Physical life ends like it began and returns to undefeated innocence.

Caregiving for someone with Alzheimer's can be painfully brutal. We know how it ends. There is no cure. It doesn't get better. But I learned that we don't have to be defeated by it.

Do you wonder where God is in Alzheimer's? Are you searching for hope in caregiving? I searched too—I lost both of my parents to Alzheimer's. They were its innocent victims.

I loved my parents with the entirety of my soul, and I anxiously awaited the moment of seeing my mom's eyes light up when I handed her a published copy of this book. But she lost her battle and gained her wings before I could have that moment. Our family's story has been raw and personal. I share it so I can tell you that I know it hurts, and I believe in you.

You are not alone—five million Americans are diagnosed with Alzheimer's, and fifteen million caregivers gave over eighteen *billion* hours of care in 2015.[1] If you feel broken, stressed, scared, scarred, tear-filled, fear-stained, and weary, I have been there. Through all of it. What started as casual caregiving became all consuming—until I could define it all as grace. I couldn't count it all joy, but I could count it all grace. And I discovered that God's unmerited favor of abundant grace could bring abundant joy.

Caregiving is an inspiring, selfless act of love. Subsequent generations are inspired by it. But I know you need more than a cheerleader. If you'll allow me to hold your hand, I'll lead you through my journey to discover grace, even in a sock drawer.

Introduction

German neurologist Alois Alzheimer began observing bizarre behavioral manifestations in a patient named Mrs. Deter, who died in 1906. After her death, Dr. Alzheimer researched her medical records and brain. He kept painstaking notes and prepared stains showing the plaques and tangles in her brain that he believed resulted in her death. The disease was first called "Alzheimer's Disease" in 1910 by a renowned colleague. However, the science community wasn't particularly interested learning about what he discovered. Dr. Alzheimer died five years later from a streptococcal infection. Decades later, in the early 1990s, critics reconfirmed through his meticulous notes and research that Mrs. Deter died of Alzheimer's Disease. Because of his research, this disease had a face and a name.

From broken memories to broken bones, Alzheimer's catalyzed terror and defeat in my family. My parents were terrorized by the scrambling of their thoughts and memories, and we who loved them had to suffocate our feelings of defeat as we watched them return to innocence.

What was terror? It was pounding on a glass door at midnight to get in from the cold and no one answered. It was driving a hundred miles to try to find the wife he could only remember from decades ago. It was begging a 911 dispatcher to take her *home* to a neighborhood from long ago. It was barging into a resident's room in the middle of the night and asking, "Where is my dead husband's body?" It was playing the starring role of a relentless daughter witnessing decades of memories slipping away. It was revealing a mama's buried secret of sexual abuse. It was the early morning phone call from the hospital. And it's a daughter's fear of passing the terror of Alzheimer's to her own children.

Through it all, I found sustenance in caregiving. It became one of the richest experiences of my life. Through grace, how we love and what we do indeed matters.

What is a Caregiver?

Do nothing out of selfish ambition or vain conceit. Rather, in humility value others above yourselves, not looking to your own interests but each of you to the interests of the others.

Philippians 2:3–4

Chapter 1

Yes, Send Me!

I have fought the good fight, I have finished the race,
I have kept the faith. Now there is in store for me the
crown of righteousness, which the Lord, the righteous
Judge, will award to me on that day—and not only to
me, but also to all who have longed for his appearing.

2 Timothy 4:7–8

"This is the nursing station. We need to talk to you about
your dad."

The phone call I always dreaded interrupted the monotonous
clicking of my keyboard and announced the beginning of my father's
final journey. He fought the good fight, and it was time for him to go
to his eternal home. Alzheimer's was finally being defeated by grace.

My coworkers began to trickle into the office, breaking the early
morning solitude. I slowly rose to close my door for this private
moment and whispered a silent prayer for strength. My tears gently
flowed, and I began to gratefully reflect on the events of his life and
our lives together before that phone call.

He valiantly served our country in the Korean War. He
entertained his fellow soldiers by playing his guitar outside his tent

and offering solace instead of fear—to himself and to his battle buddies. Dad was silent about the details of war, like so many other veterans. He was only twenty-four years old when his unit was called out to rescue badly wounded troops. Those few days of service on the front line undoubtedly changed him from a boy to a man. Those experiences instilled in him the desire to serve others and brought him to a twenty-year career as a police officer that started at the age of forty—a job he loved only slightly less than serving his family as a husband and father.

For years, my dad's animated laughter brought tears to his eyes and joy to my heart. He loved being a storyteller. He perfected the art of surprising his family and friends with seemingly true stories that were actually extended-play versions of funny jokes. Dad's charm was delightfully addictive—from serving up family pranks to carrying a gun by day and knitting needles at night to craft each of us a pair of red, white, and blue slippers. Dad bought me my first guitar, accused me of cheating when I beat him at backgammon, challenged me at cribbage, and taught me how to knit.

Signs of Alzheimer's gradually began to manifest in my dad in his early seventies. It started with little things like stammering, defining words with other words, losing things, and repeating stories more than usual. For my fiftieth birthday, my husband surprised me with a trip to Arkansas to spend time with my parents, which included Dad and me playing guitar together at the local senior center—until he could no longer remember the chords. I realized a few years later that I witnessed the defeat of his guitar by *it*. It was the last time we played music together.

Dad began telling my mom he was looking for Beverly, and he would leave for hours trying to find her. Because of the disease, he could only remember my mom as the Beverly he married in 1953, not as the wife standing loyally at his side.

As the disease continued its rampage, *it* got angry with his wife when she would try to stop him from driving. *It* became aggressive and bruising when she kept him from the car keys. *It* would get him lost a hundred miles away from home. Dad would always somehow find his way to a police station. He carried his badge, shared cop stories, and told them he was ready to return to duty. But *it* wouldn't allow him to find his way home. He couldn't remember what home was anymore.

Dad quickly lost decades of memories, and I told Mom to call me if she ever needed help. One evening at dinner time, Mom called me. "He keeps saying he just spoke with his mother a few days ago, and he's angry I won't get her on the phone. Could you talk to him, please?"

Mom gave the phone to my dad, and I said, "Hi, Dad. What's going on?"

"I just talked to my mother last week. Your mother won't give me the phone number so I can call her again."

"Dad, I'm really sorry, but your mom passed away when I was twelve years old. Grandma's been gone for forty years."

Dad didn't say much, and my heart broke for both of us. I thought he might cheer up if he could talk to his grandson. I passed the phone to my son who said, "Grandpa, how are you doing?"

"Well," said Dad, "I just found out my mom died."

Alzheimer's Disease not only robs the life out of the one who has it, it also robs the life out of the whole family. Alzheimer's took my dad, and it wasn't going to give him back.

A few months later, during another exasperated phone call from Mom, I knew I needed to rescue them both. She was at the end of her rope, her battle with depression returned, and she threatened to leave him to fend for himself. Mom courageously battled it long enough. The pain of losing my dad one day at a time was terrifying to her.

I said to Mom, "We're losing Dad, but I can't lose you too. He loves you and doesn't mean to hurt you. But *it* is hurting you, and he could kill somebody if we let him continue to drive. We have to do things differently now, Mom."

We made the difficult decision to take Dad away from the home he loved to go to a place he would never leave. Within a few days from my home in Minnesota, I found a nursing home in Arkansas that had a room for him, and I reassured Mom that I would come to move him there. I always loved flying. But on the quiet flight to Arkansas, the disease stole my joy.

Dad was excited to see me when I made my surprise arrival at the house. His beautiful blue eyes sparkled as they welled up with tears at seeing his baby girl. I never wanted his bear hug to end. My heart was breaking, and it pained my spirit to look him truthfully in the eyes. After a tearful explanation and a faithless promise that he was just trying it for a little while, we arrived at the nursing home a few hours later.

My dad could always bring humor to difficult circumstances. He joked with the nurses and administrators until they rewarded him with their laughter. He helped *us* to be at ease. But he kept saying, "Why? For how long? What did I do wrong?" Mom and I walked away that day feeling heartbroken and guilty. Our eyes were swollen from the tears, and we went back to the silent house. After twenty years, the house my dad built lost its joy—it was barren without his laughter and big personality.

Dad crossed into the late stages of Alzheimer's in February 2010. I called out to God, "Why are you allowing Dad to walk through this debilitating and hideous disease?" God instantly shared his humbling answer: "Because you aren't ready to let him go yet." How dare I be so selfish!

God gave me a vivid dream a few weeks later. I woke up with a pounding heart and the ability to remember every detail. Dad was dressed in his dark blue jeans rolled up to the ankles and a white V-neck T-shirt. In my dream he was a leaner and slightly younger version of Dad, but he was my handsome father indeed. He was beholding the bright radiant light of eternity, and gazing into the eyes of Jesus. I could see that Dad's effervescent smile and countenance were fully at peace. He was ready to enter heaven. And I was being asked to invite him to the gates.

For years I heard of people giving loved ones permission to die. I stumbled over the concept and considered it to be an oxymoron—if I truly loved someone, how could I ever tell them to die?

God helped me to finally recognize that this wasn't about me. It was all about my dad. He served in Korea and in the Minneapolis Police Department, and he served and loved his family. Dad held on because he didn't want to cause grief to his family, and he didn't want to stop serving the family he loved more than his own life.

Dad taught me how to be brave, and it was time to let him go. I coveted the courage to give my dad a final act of kindness. I was his beloved baby girl, and I had to find the compassion to tell him that when it was his time, I would be okay.

Father's Day arrived a few months later. I desperately hoped he might remember me. He always seemed to come out of the fog for me, even if just for a few moments. With Mom's help, we planned for me to call him at the nursing home.

My mom held the phone up to his ear. I told him how much I loved him. I could hear Mom telling him it was me on the phone, but his only response was gibberish and mumbling. My hope of connecting with him on Father's Day like the previous fifty years was gone. *It* had seemingly taken that away too.

Mom took the phone from my dad. He immediately shouted, "I want to talk to Cheryl!" Mom put the phone back up to his ear. My heart melted, my eyes leaked, and I once again proclaimed, "Happy Father's Day, Dad. I love you!"

He said, "You love me?"

"I sure do, Dad. Always."

Six weeks later, my husband and I traveled again to visit my parents, knowing it wouldn't be much longer. We visited Dad daily, even though he appeared to be unaware we were even there. The disease remained his captor. On the final day of our trip, we stopped at the nursing home on our way out of town and prayed he could finally come out of the fog to greet us.

We found him in the dining hall, his wheelchair pulled up to the table. He sat alone, slumped over his breakfast tray. My husband, Chuck, prayed for me from his vantage point in a far corner of the room. On this final day with the man who was my first love, I had the privilege of serving him. I sat at his side and adjusted his clothes protector (the nursing home's polite synonym for bib). Spoonful by spoonful, I assisted him in eating his oatmeal as I tenderly reminded him to chew and to swallow. I gently wiped off each morsel of oatmeal from his silent lips and flashed back to when my children were toddlers. But this was my father.

He still didn't come out of the fog.

We rolled him out to the garden gazebo, hoping perhaps the fresh air and the sound of the bubbling fountain would bring him out. I started telling Dad about my dream. I quoted his favorite scripture from John 14 about "going to prepare a place for you."

My planned talk was interrupted when his head slowly escaped from its bowed posture. His vivid blue eyes once again sparkled as he gazed at me, then at my husband, and back at me again. He had spoken nothing discernible for weeks. But with amusement and attitude, Dad said, "Hi!"

Our souls abided in the moment. My husband memorialized it with our camera. Dad and I reunited during those twenty seconds together, and I told Dad again how proud of him I was, that I loved him, and that he was a man of courage and honor.

During this moment—this gift from God—I knew that my dad knew that I loved him, and my dad knew I knew that he loved me. Then as quickly as it began, his head slumped again. That priceless moment of closure between us passed.

I voicelessly praised God for the moment and pleaded with him, *Lord, and now you want me to give him permission to die?!*

I battled my tears and, convinced he could still hear me, I told Dad that when Jesus came for him, it was okay to go home. I told him he fought hard, and that his life and his love inspired me my whole life. And I again told him, "I love you, Dad."

I rolled him back inside the nursing home. During our final, private moment, I could hardly contain my tears. I snuggled up close to him, held his hand, and gently stroked his face as I trembled with emotion. I told him he didn't need to worry about me anymore. I was married to a good man, and we would always take care of Mom. My hand felt a delicate squeeze from the protective hand that used to guide me safely across the street. Now I was helping him cross safely into heaven.

The words "I love you, Dad" and "Goodbye, Dad" came from my lips for a final time. I kissed him. I knew it was my last goodbye, and I fought to leave his side. I wanted to crawl into the safety of his tender lap one more time and ask him to wipe away my tears.

A few days later at eight o'clock in the morning, August 3, 2010, I answered the call from the nursing home in the privacy of my office.

"We haven't been able to get any response from your dad this morning. His vital signs are weak. The doctor will be here shortly. We need to know if you want us to bring him over to the hospital, or if we should put him in a comfort room." Mom and I chose the latter.

A tapestry woven with the words of Psalm 23 adorned the wall next to Dad's head as he rested peacefully on his pillow. His granddaughter and his wife kept vigil at his side. Each call I made to check on Dad over the next twenty hours became increasingly challenging for me. I learned a lot about death markers, and Dad raced quickly to the finish line. God's grace was abundant as He called my father home.

At 5:10 a.m., August 4, 2010, Dad slipped into heaven, surely dressed in his dark blue jeans rolled up to the ankles and a white V-neck T-shirt. He was lean, young, and handsome. He entered the bright radiant light of eternity, gazing only into the eyes of Jesus. His effervescent smile and countenance were now fully at peace. He entered heaven. He was invited into the gates.

7

It relinquished control of my dad. He was in God's care now. Dad fought the good fight, finished the race, and kept the faith. He received his crown in heaven.

Just weeks later, we reluctantly acknowledged that *it* now manifested in Mom. She lost her husband and gained an evil sidekick looking only to plunder her innocence.

Thus began my quest to discover what God says about caregiving for someone with Alzheimer's. I was on a mission to *find* God's strength to empower me to *give* strength to my mom. What I found was grace.

I am not a theologian or a scholar. I am a woman, wife, mother, sister, daughter, and friend, and my mom needed me the most. I was challenged to find balance between caregiving for Mom while remaining devoted to the rest of my family. I'm sharing with you my journey through the beauty, demands, rewards, and sorrows as I sought God's courage to get up every morning, regardless of whatever I needed to face, solve, or accept. You are not alone. God is only a tear or a prayer away, and I'm writing this for you.

It seemed odd to me to ask God what he could tell me about caregiving and Alzheimer's, since the term "Alzheimer's" was manmade long after the Bible was written. But because His promise of faithfulness is eternal, He unveiled a tidal wave of answers through sermons, Sunday school classes, worship songs, scripture, and the Holy Spirit. My Bible looked like a college notebook with notes scribbled *everywhere* as he began to teach me how to find and give grace.

My search began by combining the Beatitudes with the fruit of the Spirit in the order in which they are presented in Matthew and Galatians, respectively. Each chapter of *Undefeated Innocence* relates to one Beatitude (a virtuous trait embodied by Jesus) and one fruit of the spirit (a godly attribute we are to demonstrate to others), woven together with personal stories, biblical examples, and challenging wisdom. The more I studied, the more God helped me grow in my grace relationship with him and with my mom as her caregiver. He showed me that we are never defeated when we rely on him to pave the way.

God Is the Creator of Caregiving

In the beginning, God created caregivers. Adam enjoyed his role of caring for the land and animals God spoke into existence, and Eve was created to be the First Lady of Eden and a helpmate for Adam. Even when Adam and Eve were banished from the Garden of Eden for sinning against God, he promised to always care for His children. His son, Jesus Christ, was later sent to live among mankind and overcome an excruciating death so we could see and experience God's love for us. God sent his Son so you and I could share eternity in heaven with him.

Jesus is the ultimate caregiver— he shares our load and willingly sacrificed himself for us. He shows us love, joy, peace, forbearance, kindness, goodness, faithfulness, gentleness, and self-control (the fruit of the Spirit). He carries our burdens when we cannot walk or stand on our own. But his life on earth was often painful and unpleasant. He was abused, mocked, scorned, beaten down, taunted, rejected, and oppressed. He never complained. He always sacrificed. He always loves.

Jesus called the disciples to ministry and sanctification, much as you and I have been called and set apart to minister as caregivers. We lovingly sacrifice and share in the load for someone who can no longer do it alone. And sometimes we are abused, mocked, scorned, beaten down, taunted, rejected, and oppressed.

Before Jesus delivered a series of public messages known today as the Sermon on the Mount, he took the disciples aside privately to remind them that the ministry they were being called to do was about him, not about them. He appealed to them to understand that he was not only asking them to care for his flock after he was gone, but he also expected them to live out their lives exhibiting his character traits. Jesus wanted their legacies to be spiritual acts of worship passed down to future generations. By mere definition, a disciple is one who consistently practices the precepts of the one they are following. Jesus exhorted the disciples to personally display all of the virtues of what is now referred to as the Beatitudes.

Jesus challenged the disciples to authentically live out what they believed, to avoid being sidetracked by self-perceived position or power, to compassionately serve those who need help, and to lead the world to Jesus. He wanted to make sure the only thing swelling was the crowd—not the egos of the disciples! If their actions didn't match their words, they were not authentic disciples.

The Beatitudes are still regarded as a code of virtues we are to humbly follow in their entirety, as a whole, not picking and choosing one virtue to the exclusion of others. God's expectation of a caregiver is to live out an authentic faith, not to be sidetracked by the trappings of the role of guardian or caregiver, to compassionately serve those who need help, and to lead others to Jesus.

Caregiving is filled with panoramic moments of joy—singing, dancing, belly laughs, smiling, happy tears, satisfaction, closure, accomplishments, and successes of all shapes and sizes. I learned how to let my guard down and admit that when things didn't make sense, I could choose laughter instead—or a rich piece of chocolate.

Caregiving is also filled with challenges—abuse, scorn, taunting, rejection, oppression, endless errands and doctor appointments, family discord, legal proceedings, depression, lost sleep, lost jobs, lost friends, lost family, lost finances, and more.

When you live out an authentic faith, God's power manifests *within* you as you manifest the character traits of the Beatitudes, and His love manifests *through* you as you pour out the fruit of the Spirit to others. This is what I call regifting grace!

God's Calling

My parents created their dream home in the Ozarks in 1990, and Dad later expressed his desire that one of his daughters would one day live in the home their love built. At that point in my life, I couldn't fathom moving into a log home in a rustic town named Yellville, Arkansas, eight hundred miles away from the bustling suburban life in Minnesota. Did I really want to raise my two children in the land of Turkey Trot Days, Toadsuck Days, and the infamous Bean Feed and Outhouse Races? No—not me! I had a wonderful church, a lifetime in the same suburban area, lifelong friends, family, a hairstylist I liked, and a Wal-Mart in every town.

Quite frankly, I liked my life the way it was.

Sometimes we get to choose our life's mission, but sometimes our life's mission chooses us to accomplish God's will. You can now find me eight hundred miles from Minnesota suburbia, living in rustic Yellville, attending raucous festivals with strange names, and loving our log home more and more every day simply because the presence of my parents still resides here. I still have Wal-Mart, my children are college graduates, my husband and I found a new church home, and I have a new hairstylist.

Quite frankly, I like my life the way it is.

I must admit a few more gray hairs sprouted before the decision to move and become caregivers for Mom was officially made. I was afraid of radically changing the world I knew, and my husband would need to retire from a career he loved. I was apprehensive about having a backstage pass to watch Alzheimer's corrode my mom's world.

I'm not the only one called outside the comfort zone, a blissful place where all seems right with the world. I sought inspiration in godly heroes to ease me through the transition.

Moses was called to lead others to the Promised Land, a place he failed to reach himself. But through the process, God shaped him into one of history's greatest leaders.

Jabez was born out of his mother's pain. He was a seemingly minor biblical character who sparked a whole ministry movement because he prayed constantly for God to bless him, enlarge his territory, be with him, and keep him safe. Many have prayed the prayer of Jabez to be shaped by God and to be used for great purposes. He was called to do something he didn't think he could do.

Joseph led a great life as a young lad and a favored son. He sported a special coat his father gave him. His brothers threw him into a pit out of jealousy, expecting him to die. But he was spared, sold as a slave, spent time in prison, became a ruler of Egypt, and was used by God to prepare a nation for a great famine.

Queen Esther was a woman of strong character and noble beauty, and I bet she had her own hairstylist. God called her for a special purpose to courageously save her family, even though her actions could have resulted in great harm to herself.

A teenage girl named Mary was interrupted one night by a mighty angel announcing she would become the mother of the Messiah, the only one to hold him when he was born and to hold him when he died, and one of the first to see him risen from the grave.

Paul's dramatic calling by God on the Damascus Road resulted in exchanging complacency for transforming faith in so many lives. He said God works for the good of those who love him [2] and that nothing will ever separate us from God's love.[3] Those are promises I have held close in my soul, especially during the really tough days as a caregiver.

The common thread woven between these biblical heroes is that God prepares each of us uniquely because we each have a unique purpose. The calling of a caregiver is not easy. But God promises to light the path, give strength, and never leave us to fend for ourselves.

Sometimes God whispers through the soft, still voice of the Holy Spirit, and other times he shouts by showing an undeniable path.

We could see that Mom wasn't doing well, even before Dad passed away. Her depression returned, she barely ate, and the familiar forgetfulness and struggling with words was apparent. Two years after Dad passed, we moved her into a senior adult community twenty miles away from Yellville. We unsuccessfully tried to sell my parents' house, but we were able to successfully sell our comfortable home in the suburbs.

Every door that needed to shut and every door that needed to open clearly responded in a way that we could not deny was by the hand of God. In 2013, we left the land of ten thousand lakes to move to a population of thirteen hundred people (not counting hundreds of armadillos, feral pigs, possums, raccoons, copperhead snakes, and a few cute little road runners). Mom had already entered into the middle stages of Alzheimer's. At the time she passed, which was during the time I was writing *Undefeated Innocence*, she had entered advanced stage six of Alzheimer's with severe vascular dementia (caused by repetitive mini-strokes).

You and I have diverse caregiving stories. What remains identical is our heavenly Father's love and strength for us, as well as the need for us to care for ourselves in much the same way we provide care for others.

It's important to remember a flight attendant's instruction that, in case of an emergency, you need to put the oxygen mask on yourself first and then assist others. We can only be as strong for others as we are for ourselves. The greatest source of spiritual oxygen is allowing the Holy Spirit to minister in all circumstances through God's grace.

Mom suffered an exceptionally awful day when we eventually moved her from independent to assisted living. This difficult change was worsened by multiple issues with her new room. Like many people with dementia experiencing a change, she defiantly cussed, yelled, and got physically aggressive. Her pupils were constricted, and the sparkle that once graced her soft brown eyes turned rabid and cold.

I led her to her favorite chair and sat closely in front of her. My husband sat and prayed from across the room. I gently held her face in my hands and told her to keep looking at me, even as she kept looking away in her frustrated rage. I felt as if I were looking into the eyes of the devil while the Holy Spirit whispered in my ear.

There was so much tension. But I put on my oxygen mask first and prayed. I couldn't assist my mom if I wasn't connected to my own lifeline first.

A peace began to console me. I slowly and softly spoke to her, reminding her who I was, that she always trusted me to do the right thing, and that I loved her dearly. Mom's body began to relax. She no longer tried to look away from me, and she told me how much she loved me.

Losing both parents through Alzheimer's allowed me to become stronger in my faith by teaching me how to ask God the right questions and to position myself to be blown away by his grace-filled answers. You are demonstrating a courageous act of love. Others are watching. I can promise you that you are inspiring others as they witness how God is using you.

The Holy Spirit is the actual presence of God in you, providing his truth[4] and his strength.[5] He wants to encourage you in each step of this tough assignment called caregiving. Some days I could only shake my head and wonder how I could possibly make such monumental decisions. However, choosing to stand firm in my faith and calling on God's divine truth gave me the strength to keep moving forward one day at a time, step by step.

Be encouraged to find your strength in the Holy Spirit and crave to become more like Christ. In his strength, you will be divinely protected from negative distractions and equipped to be a faithful servant caregiver. Be encouraged! God has this all figured out and has appointed and anointed you personally for the job.

My caregiving prayer for you is this: If you have been placed in the position of being a caregiver, there are many others who have walked or are currently walking the same obstacle course. There will probably be times when you'll wonder where God is. It's okay to tell him that and to ask him where he is. My prayer is that he abundantly reveals himself to you in ways you'll never forget. He did it for me, even in the moments of total darkness. My prayer is that he breathes encouragement back into your soul.

Prayer: Abba Father, thank you for grace and mercy in all things to those who love you. Thank you for modeling through your Son's life on earth how to live a life filled with your virtues and attributes. For those called to be caregivers, please provide clarity and wisdom to seek your will first above all else. Teach steadfastness, and please give daily reassurance that you will never ask us to do anything we cannot do through your authority. Lord, help us to fight the good fight and run the race all the way to the finish line. Keep our faith above reproach through both the good times and the bad. Thank you for commissioning us to be conduits of your love to those who need our help. In Jesus' name. Amen.

Chapter 2

Sweet Love Story

Blessed are the poor in spirit, for theirs is the kingdom of heaven.

Matthew 5:3

But the fruit of the Spirit is love . . .

Galatians 5:22

"My Dearest One,

Just a few lines to let you know that I'm on my way. I'm in Inchin, Korea, waiting for a boat to take me to Sasebo, Japan. We should leave sometime tomorrow. It's really hard to believe that I'm finally on my way back to you. I love you so very much. Honey, I love you very much and I want you to know that you are in my thoughts all of the time. I love you with all my heart."

A letter from my dad to my mom dated April 27, 1952.

In May 1952, Private First Class Donovan Crofoot anxiously arrived home just in time from the Korean War to take Beverly, the love of his life, to her high school prom. Seven months later, my dad celebrated Christmas Eve with Beverly and her parents at their home. During that visit, he tearfully asked for my mom's hand in marriage. They married two months later on Valentine's Day of 1953. Mom was only eighteen, and Dad was twenty-four.

Their marriage was fragrantly seasoned with love. For fifty-six years, they were never apart.

Before we placed Dad into the nursing home, Mom was determined to care for him. She kept the diagnosis and severity of his Alzheimer's a secret from the rest of the family for as long as she could. She thought her love could protect him from the rampages of its progression and desperately hoped he would get better. Not even her love could coax the disease into submission, and his sundowning threatened them both.

Sundowning is a marked increase in agitation, confusion, and memory loss that appears predominantly later in the day or early evening. It frequently includes hallucinations and wandering and is one of the hallmark symptoms of the later stages of Alzheimer's. Dad's sundowning showcased his unstoppable desire to go out driving, just like in the days of our family's Sunday afternoon drives. Mom tried to take the keys away from him. But instead of a kiss goodbye, he aggressively slammed her against the refrigerator as he bolted out the door.

Dad told her, "I have to find Beverly. You're not stopping me." Mom convinced herself he was married to two women named Beverly.

Mom and I talked almost daily. It was difficult to rein in my tears as I tried to convince both of us that he really didn't mean to hurt her.

"Dad loves you so much, Mom. He is searching for *you*. He doesn't remember you the way you are now. But he's trying to find the love of his life he married on Valentine's Day," I assured her.

Mom often reached the end of her rope caring for Dad, particularly during his times of hopelessly searching for Beverly and their Minnesota home from two decades earlier. One night, he ended up at a police station a hundred miles away. It was nearly midnight when Mom got the call. She told the officer to lock him up and keep him overnight—she would be there in the morning. Dad enjoyed his sleepover at the station. He and the officers exchanged cop stories, jokes, and adventures. He had a blast, while my mom remained sleepless from worry.

When Mom told me that my dad was bruising her, I insisted it was time to end the madness. He could kill himself or others if allowed to drive anymore, and I was worried about him causing physical injury to my mom. I told her, "We can't save Dad, but I can't lose both of you." Dad went from being the one who protected and served others, especially his family, to needing his family to protect him and those around him from the terrors of his disease.

I wept over the phone with her. We were brokenhearted by the bitter reality that significant changes were no longer optional. My mom and I reached the end of our respective ropes, feeling defeated and poor in spirit. But feeling defeated and poor in spirit brought us to our knees and to the feet of Jesus in order to make wise decisions for my dad.

God didn't create us to be bogged down by the turbulent storms of life. Caregiving can be fraught with storms, including being at the end of your rope—the perception of not being able to take another step because your soul is numb from the heaviness of distress. The end of the rope is not anger, retaliation, violence, or hatred, but it requires us to expend emotional energy solely on survival and the need to find something greater than ourselves to carry the load. That's Jesus, and he leads us to his grace when we are poor in spirit. You and I don't have to do caregiving alone. He demonstrates abundant grace through the worst of storms. I needed to be willing to reach the end of myself; when I got there, he was there with an endless pitcher of grace to pour out. He has one with your name on it too.

This concept is so important that Jesus' first instruction to the disciples and the key to becoming virtuous was to be poor in spirit! He needed them to rely solely on him and his teachings, not on themselves. Jesus knew he would be calling his disciples to perform miracles, such as healing, after his ascension to heaven. The last thing Jesus wanted was for his disciples to boast about being in his inner circle and make the ministry about them. In the same way, when we rely on our own will, God can't be the sole authority—our desire for controlling our own lives supersedes God's will. When my desires supersede God's will, I get in over my head and make mistakes. My ego blinds my spiritual eyes to be able to see God's will. But my spiritual vision is 20/20 when my spirit yields to God's authority.

Our human tendency—our natural bent—is to control our own destiny, which can result in narcissism and arrogance. God wants us to be seeking him daily in everything. If we follow our natural tendency, we won't have much room for God, and our personal mission statement will become *it's all about me*, rather than *it's all about grace*.

When Dad got to the end of his rope, he relied on Mom to help him. When Mom got to the end of her rope, she relied on me. When I got to the end of my rope, I relied on God. But I needed to step aside and allow God to be sovereign in order for him to walk me through the storm. When I am poor in spirit and at the end of *myself*, only then can I fully surrender my will to *God's* will and fully trust that he can and will walk with me through everything.

As caregivers, there are plenty of times when we cannot handle it anymore. Giving up appears easier than dealing with a life that becomes a puzzle with half of the pieces missing. In those times for me, God wanted me to call out for him so he could bring heaven to me. He saw my tears, heard my cries, and felt my pain. He desired to relinquish my fear, sadness, confusion, hurt, vanity, prestige, pride, self-pity, and doubts. He wanted me to experience the tidal wave of his presence and protection.[6]

Being *poor* in spirit allows God to restore to a place of wholeness. God doesn't want to control. If he did, he wouldn't have created humanity with free will. With God, it is all about how much he wants to give, not how much he wants to control.

In contrast, the phrase "*break* your spirit" is control and destruction of a person's will. It happens through abuse, yelling, shaming, ridiculing, bullying, hitting, and withholding the necessities of life, including affection. Parents do it to children, spouses do it to each other, and employers do it to employees. It happens in boot camps, prisons, and schools. And yes, it frequently happens in caregiving.

I learned that when I'm poor in spirit and call out for God's help, God doesn't say, "How can I break you?" Instead he says, "How can I help you?" His offer of help welcomes me into his presence, and the very kingdom of heaven becomes mine. Heaven becomes my guaranteed address.[7]

When my mom was in later stages of Alzheimer's, I internalized my anger over having to give the same answers to the same questions over and over—she didn't live in a campground, she didn't have to drive the motor home, Dad went to heaven five years earlier, she lived in a safe senior community, and she was financially secure. I didn't get angry at Mom, but my blood pressure boiled over at the disease.

I experienced anguish and sadness when I couldn't just be her daughter. Sometimes I just wanted to talk to my mom. I desired the way she used to comfort me, give me wise advice, and be my biggest fan. But these frustrations distracted me from experiencing God's peaceful presence. I couldn't be poor in spirit when I made it about myself.

The First Fruit

The first three fruits of the Spirit—love, joy, and peace—are innate emotions. It's how we are supposed to feel because we were created with these emotions. They aren't dependent upon personal circumstances. And the most important is love.

A light bulb is created at a factory with all its essential parts—globe, filament, wires, stem, base, and gases. Even with all of the crucial parts, if the power source is broken or missing, the light won't shine. Our power source is the first three fruits of love, joy, and peace. Without the power source, we can't illuminate the remaining fruit—patience, kindness, goodness, faithfulness, gentleness, and self-control—that show us how we are supposed to act.

My dad drew my mom closer to him through the love letters he wrote to her from Korea. His love could reside in her. Our heavenly Father draws us closer to him through the love letters he wrote to us in his word. His love can reside in us.

God created love, and he created us out of love. His love letter in First Corinthians is often read at weddings. And since God *is* love, this familiar wedding passage came alive in me every day, giving me a glimpse into how special I am in God's eyes and showing me how I needed to treat my mom as her caregiver, just by changing *love* to *God*: God is patient and kind. He never envies, boasts, or dishonors others. God is not self-seeking nor easily angered. He keeps no record of wrongs. God does not delight in evil, but he rejoices with the truth. He always protects, trusts, hopes, and perseveres. God never fails.[8]

How can I truly know God loves me?

Because he created me.[9] Because he gave.[10] Because he wept.[11] Because he healed.[12] Because he died.[13] Because he lives.[14] Because he will never leave me.[15] Because he dwells in me.[16] Because he rescues me.[17] Because he strengthens me.[18] Because he never separates himself from me.[19]

When did I experience God's love for me?

When I called out to God in my dad's final stages of Alzheimer's to ask why he hadn't taken Dad home yet, and God telling me it was because our family wasn't ready to let him go yet.

When God gave me a vivid dream showing Dad going to heaven, with an instruction that I was to bring him to the gates of heaven.

When Dad became cognitive for the last time and fought his way out of the fog to say "Hi" and then passed into the arms of Jesus four days later.

When he brought healing into my life after abuse.

When he healed and restored my relationship with my sister.

Whenever I hurt or doubt or wonder if God's love is real, I remember these *God moments*, wipe the tears from my eyes, and feel him holding me again. I needed to frequently do that during some of the battleground times of caregiving.

In those times, it wasn't always an easy assignment to love my mom as God loved me, especially because I hated the way this disease consumed my mom. I kept emptying myself of the hatred and my selfishness in order to give Mom the unconditional love God wanted me to emulate and that she deserved.[20]

Over the years, I fell short many times of loving others in the ways God has loved me.

I grew weary with Mom because I had to explain for the hundredth time that her room was *not* a motor home, didn't have wheels, and we never moved it.

I shed tears when Mom begged to know the truth if Dad was dead and if her other husband (she was married only once) was dead too.

I grew weary of taking her to the litany of doctor appointments.

I grew weary seeing her get bitterly angry with others, even swearing in Sunday school.

I grew weary of the phone calls from the nursing home advising me that Mom was in yet another verbal altercation with another resident, and the staff returned her to her room to remind her that profane language was not acceptable.

I grew weary when Mom was confused about who I was.

And I was heartbroken when she punched a pregnant nurse in the stomach.

Despite all this, she deserved to be loved unconditionally with patience, kindness, honor, dignity, protection, trust, hope, and perseverance. She deserved to be loved unconditionally, without envy, pride, or anger, and without keeping track of the things she forgot or did. She deserved to see the presence of God in me through the way I loved her.

And what I learned most of all is that when I'm poor in spirit, there's more of God—and more of me to share love through the conduit of his love.

My caregiving prayer for you is this: I know it's hard to see someone you love need your care. Please resist the temptation to feel guilty about anything you perceive you aren't able to give. You are perhaps an advocate or caregiver because no one else volunteered to do it. No matter what condition your loved one is in, he or she will still feel your love and sense your devotion to their quality of life. You are changing a life through your love and through God's grace in your life. It was hard for me to recognize that being poor in spirit was a godly virtue. But when I allowed God's presence to permeate my soul, I could love my mom more deeply.

~~~~~~~~~~~~~~~~~~~~~~~~

Prayer: Lord, you are a good, good Father. Your love is unlike any other and eternally mine. When I feel lost, hungry, broken, or thirsty, you promise to guide me out of the anguish. When I cry out to you because I can't find my way out of the storm, you quiet the storm to a child's whisper and lead me to a safe harbor. You turned desert into water, parched ground into flowing springs, and fields into fruitful harvest. You promise to rescue me out of affliction. I rejoice in your love for me, and I know you carry me in the palm of your glorious hand. Thank you for choosing and equipping me for your task of love. In Jesus' name. Amen. [21]

Chapter 3

Good Grief! And What's Your Name Again?

Blessed are those who mourn, for they will be comforted.

Matthew 5:4

But the fruit of the Spirit is . . . joy . . .

Galatians 5:22

I was tentative about studying what Jesus says about mourning, despite his promise to bring me comfort through it. It opened my understanding that Jesus was not only talking about mourning over the loss of a loved one, but also for those who were lost spiritually. Even so, my focus will be on you as a caregiver and the extended season of mourning that comes with Alzheimer's.

Losing the soul mate I had in my mom placed me in a season of grieving, and my initial fear was that studying mourning and grief would stir up more sadness. Jesus said that those who mourn will be comforted. I knew I needed comforting and was willing to face my fear of frailty to get it.

My study began with asking God how mourning could be a heavenly virtue. Grief hurts. Caregiving hurts. Fortunately the ultimate intent of the Beatitudes is to bring us into the presence of God. Jesus wants to partner with us in our grief. He says he will turn our mourning into gladness and bring us closer to God's comfort as an avenue to release our grief. I don't believe God promises to instantly reward us with comfort when we mourn, but he promises to walk with us through it.

My husband and I started making daily phone calls to Mom in early 2014, even though we only lived twenty miles away. We wanted to give her the gift of our familiar voices so she could have moments of normalcy amidst the chaos. And we needed the peace of mind to know she was okay.

My husband called to greet her every morning with a lighthearted, "This is your coffee buddy Chuck." She often responded with a school-girl giggle, delighted to receive his call. He helped her determine what day it was, reminded her to put in her teeth and go down for coffee, and talked about the day's upcoming events—perhaps bingo, exercise class, or ice cream. I called her every evening so she could talk about her day and hear my voice, and I could verbally tuck her in for the night. I helped her release agitation or fear by calmly talking things out or, as a last resort, making her laugh hysterically with a version of my Dad's sense of humor. Those evening calls became increasingly tough when she entered the sixth stage of Alzheimer's, and sundowning became her newest roommate.

I remember the first time I lost my mom to *it* during one of the nightly phone calls. Mom always knew who I was and my place in the family. On this night, however, the loss was oppressive. She was always my biggest fan, and now I was merely a stolen memory.

"Hi, Mom. This is your daughter Cheryl."

"I'm so glad you called," Mom said. "I'm really mixed up today. How many daughters do I have?"

"You have two, and I'm your daughter Cheryl."

"Where do they live?"

"I'm your daughter Cheryl, we live in Yellville, and your other daughter lives in New York."

"I have another question. Who takes care of my daughters?"

"We are both grown up now, Mom, and no one is taking care of us. I'm fifty-seven years old."

"Oh," she said. "And what's your name again?"

I knew this stage would come, and I dreaded facing the juncture that would forever change the landscape of our relationship. I battled my tears, as well as the urge to throw my phone against the wall. I ultimately chose to suck it up. I knew it wasn't her fault—it was the disease. I silently prayed for help to focus only on my mom. My innocent hope that Mom would always remember me was abandoned in that phone call. Asking her to remember me when she couldn't even remember the details of her own life was probably a lofty ideal. Sometimes, technology of monitors and video cameras helped us put the pieces together of her Humpty Dumpty existence.

Only a few nights prior to that phone call, around midnight my mom opened her door, scanned the empty hallway, and hoped to find someone to help her locate my dad. Seeing none of the nurses, she desperately went to each of the security doors nearest to her room, repeatedly trying to force each door open so she could get outside. She pounded and cussed. When those attempts failed, she decided she needed to go room by room to find him.

She pounded on residents' doors and tried every door knob until she found one that opened. She escorted herself into the sleeping resident's room, who had moved in only a few days earlier, and stood at her bedside screaming, "They said my husband is dead. But tell me what you did with his body!"

The terror of Alzheimer's is contagious. Mom was terrorized by a disease she didn't want, and she spread the terror to an innocent resident, as well as to my husband and me when we got the terse phone call from the nurses. This was a significant plunge deeper into the disease, and *it* stole a larger chunk of my gentle-hearted mom. We were losing Mom, and we didn't like it at all.

Several years earlier, our adult children lovingly supported our decision to be closer to Mom, saying *she* needed us more than *they* did. They all missed us, and we missed them. But they understood.

When we moved to Arkansas, we promised our children we would annually return to celebrate an early Christmas with them. We cherished those moments with our family. On what turned out to be my mom's final Christmas in 2016, however, I stayed back in Arkansas with my mom and missed out on seeing any of our children. But I received instead a priceless gift in creating the memory of giggling with Mom as we sang Christmas carols in church together, side by side, arm in arm, and badly out of tune.

Whenever Chuck and I traveled, including in December for early Christmas celebrations, we continued to diligently make the daily calls to Mom, even if they were in front of our children.

My mom and I weathered two arduous phone conversations in front of our children during the Christmas trip in 2014. I called her early on Monday night to remind her that her friends Chuck and Rosie were coming to pick her up for a Christmas dinner at church.

"They called, but I told them I wasn't going," Mom defiantly told me.

"Mom, you were looking forward to it, and we arranged it all for you. What changed your mind?"

"I *don't* want to go. I had a great time with my *friends* today. Nobody else cares about me. I have no family. I just want to sit here and be alone."

My heart broke. "Mom, you have a lot of family who loves you."

She said, "Nobody ever comes to see me. I don't have any family."

"Mom, you are surrounded by pictures of all the family members who love you." I reminded her one by one, name by name.

"Well, they never come. I'll just sit here until I die," she said matter-of-factly.

I took a breath and silently prayed. I spoke softly and slowly to her, reminding her how much she was loved. I wanted more than anything to be able to comfort her—and to be comforted.

I can't remember my exact words that night, but her agitated voice was replaced with sweetness. Mom thanked me for loving her so much, for moving to Arkansas, and for helping her remember. The situation was diffused, and I praised God for giving me the words to settle the dust of her broken memory. But I silently began to mourn—the slow goodbye of Alzheimer's was settling in for a long winter's nap.

On the following Thursday night, the heinous lies of Alzheimer's appeared again. It was the last night with our children and young grandchildren before returning to Arkansas, and again they heard what Alzheimer's sounded like. Our grandchildren could see in my face how I was struggling with such intimate sadness. I worried for them—and for my mom as I asked her how she was doing.

"Not good at all. What am I doing here anyway?" she said with a bite in her voice.

I said, "You live there, Mom. You're in Arkansas."

"Well," she began, with a pause. "Why am I here? I want to be dead. Today was the day I was supposed to be dead. Can you tell me why I can't be dead?"

Our children saw my tormented expression as I silently called out to God to give me the words to say. I needed to help Mom, yet I didn't want to upset them. What I really wanted was to find refuge for my tears in a pillow. I excused myself into another room, took a breath, quietly prayed, and spoke softly and slowly to Mom in order to once again diffuse her emotional pain.

In this moment with my *own* grief and loss, I needed to empathize with *her* grief and loss—the loss of memories, the loss of family she couldn't always remember, and the loss of independence. God says blessed are those who mourn. Well, Lord, I was grieving, and my mom was grieving, and we both needed comfort.

I told Mom that Jesus unconditionally loved her and had an appointed time for her to be with him, but I still needed her with me. I told her I deeply loved her and was blessed to have her with me. My mom's voice steadied, as did mine. We both grieved, and we both found comfort.

Jesus passionately loved his disciples. He knew they were grieving over his imminent departure because they undeniably loved him too. Jesus used the analogy with them that when a woman is in labor, her pain is excruciating. However when the baby is born, the mother replaces the pain with great joy. Jesus promised his disciples that their grief, in much the same way, would return to joy when he returned.[22] God's promise is that great pain will be balanced with great joy.

Decades ago my mom told me how she felt right after I was born. She described how she held me up to God and sensed him telling her, "This one's special." She often told me how special I was to her and to others, especially because of my caregiving. After she passed, I found a priceless picture of her cradling me in her arms in the hospital shortly after I was born. I didn't remember ever having seen that picture before. But God used that moment of me finding it to illustrate his comfort as I grieved the earthly loss of my mom— great pain and great comfort. In caregiving, I was willing to mourn while I comforted my mom, and now God comforted me *through* my mom after her death.

Jesus bore profound grief during his earthly ministry. He developed deep relationships with Lazarus and his sisters, Mary and Martha. The sisters sent word to Jesus that Lazarus was gravely ill. He exhorted the sisters to trust because Lazarus' condition was meant for God's glory.[23]

Two days later, Jesus told his disciples that they needed to return to Bethany. The disciples rebuked Jesus out of fear for their safety because the Jews there were threatening to stone Jesus. Despite the disciples' concerns, Jesus told them Lazarus had fallen asleep, and he was going there to wake him. The disciples displayed their fear-filled aloofness when they suggested to Jesus that they ought to just let Lazarus sleep so he could get better. I can only imagine their awkwardness when Jesus told them that Lazarus was dead! The disciples feared the same fate for themselves.

Lazarus was entombed for four days by the time Jesus reached Bethany. Mary was so distraught by his death that only Martha went to meet Jesus when he arrived just outside of town.

Jesus tried to comfort her. "Your brother will rise again."

Martha returned to Mary and said, "The teacher is here and is asking for you." Mary and some of the Jews mourning with her rushed to see Jesus. Mary fell at his feet and said, "Lord, if you had been here, my brother would not have died."[24] She and the Jews began to weep, and Jesus was deeply troubled.

He asked them where Lazarus was buried, and they offered to take him there. Jesus began to weep. He wasn't just exhibiting sadness over Lazarus' death. He wept because he saw the tears of Mary and the others who came with her. He wept because they didn't trust in his promise to resurrect Lazarus. He wept because they discounted his efforts to comfort them. I believe Jesus weeps for us too—in our grief, mourning, and unbelief. He prefers to comfort rather than to wipe away tears.

As caregivers, we experience great sadness on a perpetual basis. Disease robs us of the futures we expect to have with our loved ones. We grieve the loss of time with family, friends, and finances. Mom and I were able to share in a few silly moments in her final days. But I grieve the loss of her stories, laughter, memories, mobility, understanding, and unwavering support for me.

One night I dreamt that Jesus held a placard that read, "Take Joy! I am who I say I am." The dream came during a difficult time as we sought legal guardianship of Mom. Not only was the legal battle a difficult one, but I fought back the heartbreak over the loss of my mom's ability to care for herself. God's admonition through my dream not only brought me through the legal battle, but it was a tremendous life lesson. He reminded me to trust him in the impossible times of grief, mourning, and unbelief.

Caregiving creates copious hours of sacrifice and grieving. Sleep deprivation, lost finances, lost relationships, lost time, legal battles, family battles, work issues, and abuse all take their toll on us. Perhaps you wish things could be the way they used to be or feel you are all alone. Maybe no one else is willing or able to do what you are doing. Despite the many gains of spending this special time caring for someone else, there is mourning and grief—while your loved one is alive and when your loved one has passed away. It's normal, it's painful, and Jesus knows your grief because he experienced it too.

According to Elisabeth Kübler-Ross, the five recognized stages of grief are denial, anger, bargaining, depression, and acceptance.[25]

Denial is a refusal to recognize truth or reality ("This is *not* Alzheimer's"). Anger is a warning something emotionally or mentally hurts ("I hate this stupid disease"). Bargaining is an attempt to swap something in exchange for something else ("God, if you give me one more coherent moment with her, I promise to . . ."). Depression is a condition of emotional sorrow and desolation ("What am I supposed to do now that he's gone?"). Acceptance is the acknowledgment of reality ("Time to take the car away").

Everyone goes through the stages of grief differently—different order, different timetable, different appearance. But grief and mourning are normal. Knowing these stages can help us walk through them and allow us to find comfort through them. We only run into a problem if we sign up for an extended stay visit in any of the five stages.

During Alzheimer's and other terminal illnesses, the stages of grief manifest before death because we actually lose our loved ones over the course of many weeks, months, or years, and we know the ultimate conclusion. The adage that no one survives Alzheimer's is true. I discovered, however, that the stages of grieving the gradual loss of Mom through the disease were different from the grieving I experienced after holding her hand for the very last time.

It was agonizing when my mom entered the late stages. I tried to deny the pain when she couldn't remember who I was, and I frequently wondered if I could have done something differently. It was harder to be a daughter than it was to be a caregiver. I careened through the stages of grief, bargaining with God to spare my mom and let her go home to heaven.

God promises to give us comfort as we comfort others, particularly as we advocate for them and help them feel safe amidst a horrifying disease. My mom was rightfully quite scared as this disease overpowered her, and it was scary for me. But God is the "God of all comfort, who comforts us in all our troubles, so that we can comfort those in any trouble with the comfort we ourselves receive from God."[26]

During the eye-opening phone call described at the beginning of this chapter, I anguished over the loss of my mom's ability to remember my name and her confusion as to who was taking care of me. At that moment, she could only remember me as the child she once held in her arms. It was a stepping stone to the end of her broken path, and I knew her memory of me as her adult daughter would soon begin to fade. I mourned that receiving comfort from my mom, my biggest fan, would be coming to an end.

Minutes after that phone call, my husband and I decided we would watch the movie *God is Not Dead*. We knew the basic premise of the movie, but we didn't know the details.

Within the first five minutes of the movie, there is a scene where an adult daughter is caring for her mother who has Alzheimer's. The mother looks up at her daughter, smiles, and asks, "Who are you again?" At that moment, the look of horror on the daughter's face mimicked my own. My husband comforted me with tears in his eyes as he turned to see the floodgates ready to open in mine.

Lord, how can you put me through that? I silently prayed. *How are you going to help me walk through this one?*

Was I being like Mary and Martha in their unbelief? Had I forgotten that Jesus showed me in my dream that he is who he says he is? God allows us to be honest with him and to come to him just as we are, including when we suffer authentic anger in our times of grief.

God is Not Dead is a powerful story focused on a young college student who receives a class assignment from an atheist professor to prove whether God exists. At one point, one of the characters proclaims that God's strength alone will carry us through every circumstance, and that we are to be without fear. The words screamed at me and felt like they were intended for me to hear that night. I knew God was answering my prayerful question—His strength alone would be enough to walk through any situation with Mom. God brought me comfort in this *coincidental* entertainment choice for a *coincidental* evening of sorrow.

God clearly made a covenant to comfort us in all of our present afflictions, and he guarantees we will be permanently comforted through eternity. He comforts us in order to free us from a broken heart so we can receive and give joy, the second fruit of the Spirit.

True joy is abiding in the Holy Spirit through all circumstances— the assurance that we belong to God by grace and can be free from fear. I can choose joy if I keep my emotional compass pointing toward God. Paul reflected joy, even during persecution. He said, "I have learned to be content whatever the circumstances. I know what it is to be in need, and I know what it is to have plenty. I can do all this through him who gives me strength."[27]

Joy and happiness are not equivalents. Happiness is only a prelude to joyful moments, totally dependent on external events. Happiness masquerades in a morning cup of delicately brewed coffee or a gooey chocolate chip cookie. Once the pleasure is gone, so is the happiness. Joy is eternal; happiness is fleeting.

God is filled with joy when he looks upon you because you are one of his prized creations with whom he is well pleased. He allows you to experience great joy because he first experienced joy in creating you!

Over a decade ago, I went for a long walk along a rugged creek bed. I was mesmerized by a family of ducks frolicking in the water.

I've seen plenty of ducks in my lifetime, but on that day, they uniquely captured my attention and were irresistible to watch. I watched them dive, chase, play, and swim with each other. I laughed and was filled with delight, knowing God must be taking great delight in them too. After all, he created them.

And then it hit me: Since God could find joy in the ducks he created, how much more pleasure he must be taking in me, a masterpiece created in his own image! I felt so treasured by my heavenly Father.

At that time, I was involved in a prison ministry at a level-four men's correctional facility. Some of the men were there for life because of the heinous crimes they committed. But I was moved to share my duck experience with them during one of our worship services in order to give an example of just how much God treasures all of us. A few weeks later, I recounted my story to others at church. They laughed hysterically imagining me sharing a message to lifers about ducks playing in the water, especially after I told them I received a few strange glances from some of the inmates!

Regardless of circumstance, we all need the message of truth that God finds joy in each of us. He created us and promises to fill us with his joy through the presence of the Holy Spirit, especially in difficult times. When we mourn, God mourns with us and brings us comfort. And through his comfort, we receive his joy.[28] God wants us to be filled with joy in order to regift that joy to those around us, particularly those who receive our care.

Significant personality changes are a symptom that Alzheimer's has progressed to stage six. In this stage, loved ones become more childlike, find happiness in uncomplicated things, and use simpler words. On the flip side, they also get confused and agitated when they start getting tired, have panic attacks, and throw tantrums when they can't have their way or have forgotten how to complete a familiar task, like laundry. Trying to explain to my mom that dish soap was not a good alternative to laundry detergent brought out the evil side of the disease, as did trying to convince her that no one stole her teeth.

People with dementia love music because it emotionally brings them back to an easier time. It's easy to focus on the things they can't do anymore. So instead of grieving the losses, I chose to pursue joy. I bought Mom a radio.

It's been said that since music impacts both sides of the brain, people with Alzheimer's will respond to it much longer than any other mode of stimulus. I'm amazed when I hear a song from my youth and can still sing every single word of the lyrics. In later stages, my dad lost the ability to communicate, but he continued to play his guitar until he could no longer remember the chord structures. Glen Campbell's story is similar—he forgot words to a song before he forgot how to play the music.

I went on a mission to find an old-fashioned radio without all the confusing additional features like a compact disc player, equalizer, and alarm clock—we just needed an on/off switch, a channel changer, and a volume control. I finally found one and brought it back to her room. Mom and I have always loved music, and we tuned to an oldies station on her new radio.

Not only did our faces light up to the songs we heard, but we both started singing the lyrics, belting them out with confidence as we began to dance together. "You Light Up My Life" never sounded so good! Well, in our minds, anyway.

We shared joy that afternoon. We focused on what she could enjoy, not the things she didn't understand anymore. The radio brought happiness, but the music brought back the joy of an easier era in my mom's life. She loved her new radio until she could no longer remember how to operate it. We discovered she'd just unplug it when she went to bed and then not remember why it didn't work in the morning. But at least for a while, her room was filled with joy and song—and occasional dancing!

Reminiscing about the happy moments my mom and I shared is comforting to me. We always enjoyed laughing together and even managed to act silly in church. When Mom, Dad, and I took a driving trip to California, my mom and I jogged around a campground while I wore my dad's hole-filled, smelly tennis shoes. Years later, we spent a whole evening at a car dealership test driving every car model on the lot. One by one, as we drove and returned one vehicle, the car salesman handed us the keys for the next. However when we got to the rip-roarin' Mazda RX7, he chose to go along with Mom as I stayed in the showroom. Mom didn't buy the RX7, but we each bought a car from the handsome salesman. It wasn't about what we did, but it was all about how complete we felt by embracing the moments together.

Mom and I experienced joy together because the foundation of our relationship was built on love and trust, even when she forgot my name. We were strength for each other, and we comforted each other. The car-driving event brought us happiness at the moment and still gives me joy because of what that experience meant to the fullness of our relationship.

My relationship with Jesus is the same. I feel happiness when he answers a specific prayer, but I feel joy because the foundation of his relationship with me is built on love and trust. I can always count on him. My joy is made complete because of who he is and not because of what he gives me.

Mom relied on my strength and comfort, especially during her final week of life. I can either choose to grieve the loss of no longer creating new fun times together, or I can embrace the moments of joy with Mom—like singing and dancing in her room, or reading to her the same bedtime story that she used to read to me (she still remembered some of the words).

My husband and I created a memory book for Mom filled with pictures and brief stories of her life. It was a tool we could use with Mom to help her remember her family, at least while we looked at it with her. Less than twenty-four hours after giving it to her (with a lot of pomp and circumstance), she forgot we were even there to give it to her. But the photos brought her joy because the feelings represented in those pictures were of love, strength, and trust.

My caregiving prayer for you is this: Caregiving is filled with mountaintop experiences, as well as sadness in the valleys. Through my life and through my study, I am absolutely convinced God cares about the details of my life, he allows me to mourn so he can bring me comfort, and joy is meant to be shared. Having exuberance for life is contagious, and I want you to catch it!

Prayer: Thank you, Lord, for bestowing comfort and strength during times of grieving and mourning. Thank you for bringing me back to joy as you gently remind me that you are who you say you are. You are my Shepherd and Provider. You lead me into the calm eye of the storm. And you never abandon me. Even though I sometimes walk through dark times, I know you always guide me out of them, even if the path is rugged. I refuse to live in fear, because I know you are right beside me to protect and comfort me. Even in the midst of loving someone with Alzheimer's, you anoint and equip me. Thank you for filling my life to overflowing with joy. Thank you that I can dwell with you forever. In Jesus' name. Amen.[29]

Chapter 4

Find Your Stone, Throw It Well

Blessed are the meek, for they will inherit the earth.

Matthew 5:5

But the fruit of the Spirit is . . . peace . . .

Galatians 5:22

My eyes wells up when I visit my parents in their final resting place because I miss the physical experience of the gentleness of their souls and the authenticity of their love. However, I'm grateful they no longer suffer and that I can still experience their bodacious sense of humor through the wacky variant of my own.

On a perfect September morning, after my dad joined the ranks of heaven but before my mom passed, I careened through the familiar hills of the Ozarks to reach a sole destination—Fairview Cemetery. I was resolute in purpose. I was going to find my stone.

After legendary football player and sportscaster Frank Gifford passed away, his wife Kathie Lee Gifford gave a faith-filled tribute about him on her nationally televised morning show. She described how Frank came from humble beginnings, born during the peak of the depression. He lived in twenty-nine different places before entering Bakersfield High School and sometimes ate dog food for dinner. His mother exhibited a consistent legacy of faith through those leanest of times, and Frank and Kathie Lee vowed to pass that legacy to their children, Cody and Cassidy.

During an intimate tour of the Holy Land, the Giffords were taken to the historic Valley of Elah where, centuries earlier, a meek shepherd boy named David volunteered to muster up the courage to do battle against a vicious titan named Goliath.

David methodically searched for five unmatched stones for his handcrafted slingshot, even though he trusted he would need only one to release Goliath from his vile existence. David catapulted the first stone, knocking the ogre to the ground and leaving him breathless. David then took Goliath's own sword and beheaded him. Meek David relied on his trust in God to provide him with strength and protection to slay the giant.

God had undoubtedly placed a calling on David to be a leader. When David defeated Goliath with only one of the chosen stones, he was officially commissioned to begin the calling God placed on his life. God continued to use David during his lifetime, despite his many sins, because he meekly sought forgiveness, willingly accepted the consequences of his sins, and authentically desired God's presence through his calling. God referred to him as a man after His own heart.

When the Giffords visited the place where David selected his stones, they were told to choose stones to bring back home with them to pass down as a faith lesson to their children. Frank and Kathie Lee gave each of their children one of the stones from the Valley of Elah and asked them to consider what their stone represented (the calling to use their spiritual gifts) and where and when God wanted them to throw it to change the world (the commissioning). Frank and Kathie Lee encouraged their children to discover their calling and transform the world like David did—with meekness, strength, and extreme faith.

As part of her loving tribute to Frank, Kathie Lee encouraged her viewers to pick up a stone in remembrance of God's unique calling on their lives, and then live out the rest of their lives throwing their stone as a gift to change the world.

Frank made egregious mistakes in his life, in many ways similar to David's. But both men adhered to an unwavering faith and genuinely sought forgiveness from God for their iniquities. Kathie Lee said her husband passed away in complete peace because he knew he had made the world a better place. He shared the gifts God gave him with the world. My thought is that Frank had the gift of faith which he publicly (and likely privately) demonstrated through the trials and circumstances of his life.

There are a number of online resources to help determine spiritual gifts, and it can also be beneficial to ask trusted friends and family for insight or confirmation. My spiritual gifts are mercy, faith, and prophecy. God called me to use those gifts through writing, speaking, and teaching, which have been the desires of my heart since fourth grade. Being called to use those gifts in caregiving for my parents, however, took me a little by surprise.

I got a peek at my calling on my mom's 75th birthday, just a few years before we made the decision to move to Arkansas. Like other years, I looked forward to my annual phone call and the joy of hearing her childlike laughter as I annoyed her with a rousing, off-key rendition of "Happy Birthday." What I heard instead was her deep sadness, anger, and tears. The reality of my dad's illness grieved her heavily.

With absolute clarity, I could no longer ignore how sick my dad had become—he and my mom could no longer manage his care by themselves and needed me to intercede on their behalf. Dad was rapidly losing decades of memory and manifesting risky behaviors, and Mom's trepidation was returning her deep into the recesses of depression. I was afraid they would physically hurt each other.

I couldn't predict what the future would look like, but I trusted God to travel the road with me and transform my faith forever. That day, I metaphorically picked up my stone. I accepted that I was the one to closely walk the painful journey with my parents, make their world a little bit better, and encourage others like you with God's abundant grace. Throwing my stone initially meant caregiving for those I loved and later daring to live out my lifelong passion for writing, speaking, and teaching.

Thirty minutes scarcely passed before I contacted my mom's psychiatrist and talked his nurse into squeezing my parents into his overcrowded schedule. They drove themselves to their appointment with the doctor (a true miracle in itself because it was 150 miles away). Dr. Bradley called me at the end of the consultation to relay the abysmal news that my dad was in late stages of Alzheimer's, needed immediate twenty-four-hour care, and probably had only a year to live.

Within six days, I located a care facility, tackled logistical issues, arranged for time off from work, secured airfare and a rental car, arrived in Yellville, and completed my dad's painful move. The planning and implementation were easy. Putting my emotions on the back burner to accomplish the task was the toughest. But God fulfilled his promise to give me abundant strength. The staff at the faith-based care facility not only served and loved my dad during the year he lived there, but they also served and loved our entire family. They served us in meekness, even when the ugliness of Alzheimer's manifested in Dad's aggressive behaviors against the staff.

When my dad passed a year later, it was already apparent that my mom showed symptoms of Alzheimer's. We immediately tried to write it off as grief, sadness, aging, and stress. Anything but *it*. However, we couldn't ignore the indisputable symptoms. She started losing the ability to put sentences together and could no longer remember the familiar trip to Little Rock to see Dr. Bradley (she thought we were traveling to St. Paul, Minnesota).

Fast forward now to my September drive to Dad's final resting place so I could find my stone. God had already given me my spiritual gifts and selected my calling, but it was time for me to choose a special stone to hold in my hands. When I arrived at Dad's tombstone, I felt God's presence. I looked around for the perfect stone and found it hiding near my dad's bronze service star grave marker.

I admit I expected a royal ceremony filled with pomp and circumstance, perhaps a choir of angels singing "Amazing Grace," or at least a huge rush of emotion. It sounds silly now, but I expected to feel like Paul on the Damascus Road, or at least hear a triumphant trumpet blast. When none of that happened, I questioned if I selected the wrong stone. But it wasn't the wrong stone—it was a wrong attitude.

David sought his stones knowing it would require only one. It was about having an authentic faith for a divine purpose, not the size or color of the stone, or how many. The stones both David and I selected were merely symbolic of our submission to the calling God placed on our lives. I often glance at my stone and gently weep over it because it is a reminder of *who* is really in control and what he gave me to do. Like David's, my stone is a representation of my willingness to be called and my response to meekly obey.

When I asked God to show me what the Bible says about Alzheimer's, how to be encouraged in a labored time of loving and caring for someone with Alzheimer's, and how to encourage others, his response was clear. "Then I heard the voice of the Lord saying, 'Whom shall I send? And who will go for us?' And I said, 'Here am I. Send me!'"[30]

It was an interesting choice that after Frank Gifford passed, his wife described him as a meek man. He played professional football for twelve years, was inducted into the Pro Football Hall of Fame in 1977, and became an Emmy-award winning sportscaster known best for his broadcasting on *ABC's Monday Night Football*, *Wide World of Sports*, and the Olympics. He held prominence in the world's eye and much sin and sorrow in his personal life, including a highly publicized marital betrayal. He humbly sought forgiveness and was willing to accept the consequences.

David was a meek teenager and an uncomplicated shepherd with a simple slingshot when he was taunted by and slayed Goliath. As King David, he was an exceptional military strategist and was undeniably loyal to Saul. He loved God and trusted him in battle and in victory. He was determined and courageous, but he harbored grievous sin and sorrow in his personal life. He humbly sought forgiveness from God for betrayal, deception, adultery, murder, and other sins, and he accepted the consequences.

Moses came from a humble beginning. He was adopted as an infant by the Pharaoh's daughter after he took a gentle float down the Nile River in a reed basket. He grew up in the palace, but he fled when the Pharaoh mercilessly ordered his execution. God summoned Moses in a burning bush and revealed that he was to lead the Hebrews to the Promised Land of Canaan. During forty years of wandering through the desert, he crossed through the Red Sea, received the Ten Commandments, smashed the tablets written by God because the Hebrews had built a golden calf, and relied on daily manna. Moses died at the age of 120, never having reached Canaan, presumably as punishment for not trusting God to bring water out of a rock. He is remembered as an incredible leader, yet he is described as meek and soft-spoken. [31]

Jesus was a humble servant sent from heaven to save the world and to fight for us against the powers and forces of evil.[32] He was crucified on a tree and conquered death after fighting the evil forces for three days. He was always without sin.

The above examples show four humble and meek men who maintained a controlled strength. Meekness is described as suffering injury with patience and without resentment, showing a gentle and humble nature, and not being easily provoked. Meekness is never about weakness or retaliation. Frank, Moses, and David were called to transform the world, despite their flaws and failings. They endured much, sought forgiveness when they failed, and relied on God for strength. Jesus also endured much and is the epitome of enduring injury with patience and without resentment. He was never haughty or proud, and he willingly conquered death to pay the price of our failures.

Through his example, Jesus taught his disciples to be meek. One way to comprehend meekness is to identify its opposites, which include disobedience, agitation, stubbornness, depravity, or uninhibitedness. I don't think anyone would see Jesus in me if I displayed those horrendous character flaws, nor would those traits bring me into God's presence! With meekness, even the most difficult days can be tenderized. As a caregiver, life manager, and guardian for Mom, I was to be a meek servant in all situations, including the challenging ones. I learned that in formidable situations, it was better to diffuse them rather than toil in them just to prove myself right.

It was difficult when my mom couldn't remember a special day we shared together, forgot my name, told me she wanted to be dead, was convinced someone came in and stole her glasses, or yelled at me to leave. I lamented when my mom told other residents she had no family and no one ever came to visit her. It was frustrating to second guess the nursing staff when my mom was convinced no one gave her nighttime pills or fed her meals. And it was embarrassing to hear her boldly cuss in Sunday school class because some man was sitting in her chair.

Despite everything, she was my beloved mama. She deserved my gentleness and tender spirit to tame her dragons. It wasn't her fault—it was the disease. That's when I developed two methods to help me diffuse her anxiety attacks. The nursing staff appreciated knowing they could call me anytime to talk her down from her pinnacle of panic.

~~~~~~~~~~

Diffuse Method One (internal): Pause. Pray. Respond.

I learned it was much easier to diffuse a situation by pausing to take a deep breath, praying and reflecting, and then calmly responding. These three steps allowed me to compassionately tell her that there were are a lot of people she could visit in her nursing home, remind her with pictures of the loyal family members who loved her, and reassure her no one was stealing her things or refusing to feed her.

I could explain why she needed to use soap in the shower despite the dreaded wrinkles all over her face (she forgot she was aging and was convinced the moisturizing soap was viciously adding to her gentle wrinkles). I could peacefully remind her I would help search for a missing item that apparently ran away. If she was upset over another doctor appointment, I could reassure her that the eye injections would save her vision, and the MRI might help us know how to better take care of her. That worked most of the time.

But caregivers must always be prepared to be stumped! One caregiver recently told our social media support group that her loved one liked to sneak and stash food, and she wanted our help in solving the mystery of the missing meatloaf. I kindly suggested she check the underwear drawer! More on that later!

~~~~~~~~~~~~~~~~~~~~

Diffuse Method Two (external): The Mirroring Technique.

I found that if I exhibited the placid behavior I wanted her to emulate, she would calm down. When she was agitated and talking fast and loud, I displayed meekness by slowing down my rate of speech, lowering the pitch and volume of my voice, looking right into her eyes, and speaking calmly. When I acted meekly and kept eye contact with her, Mom subconsciously mirrored meekness and returned to speaking slowly, softly, and calmly.

My mom loved when I referred to myself as her life manager and explained I took care of her finances and advocated for her medical care. Most importantly, I impacted her emotional state of being.

Most people with Alzheimer's fall into one of two categories—extremely complacent and withdrawn, or agitated and angry. Both of my parents exhibited the latter. Meekness elicits meekness, and it is a marvelous trait to use in order to diffuse difficult emotions. As Mom's life manager, I told myself to seek to be meek and to dwell on the characteristics of meekness, such as humility, patience, kindness, submissiveness, a lack of pretention, genuineness, and gentleness.

Do you sometimes struggle to hold it together? When it happens to me, I gird myself in the courage of Moses and David to face difficulty with tenacity and humility. Meekness provides strength and teaches us how to press into God. First Corinthians 13 says love is the most excellent way because it paves the way to Jesus. So does meekness.

In caring for my mom, embracing meekness helped me locate flashes of peace in the moments of turbulence. It brought me *closer* to Jesus because I became more *like* Jesus. What happens if we put too much air and pressure in a balloon? It pops. Without meekness, the pressure builds up in me and I emotionally break. Embracing meekness deflates the pressure.

It's okay to fight with a disease like Alzheimer's or cancer—for a season. There were plenty of times I wanted to kick the daylights out of that foul disease for stealing both my parents. Instead, ultimately God wanted me to adorn myself with the virtue of meekness, moving forward with gentleness and resiliency. It is better to *diffuse* than to be *right* or to *fight*. I don't want to inhibit others or myself from encountering intimacy with God.

Many people perform regular detoxes or cleansings to regain better physical health and remove poisonous toxins from the body, particularly the liver, which build up over time. Removing physical toxins can be a harsh experience—with headaches, fatigue, weakness, rashes, gastrointestinal issues, or depression. In other words, we feel lousy before we feel better.

Similarly, purging spiritual toxins like arrogance, pride, self-gratification, stubbornness, jealousy, and unforgiveness is necessary in order to maintain spiritual health. These toxins can drop into our spirit like a cat jumping on the countertop when no one is watching—we don't see it happening, but we see the destruction left behind. Spiritual toxins hinder the ability to fully abide in God's grace and abundance, and they must be continually purged. Like physical toxins, spiritual toxins accumulate without us even recognizing them until something is unhealthy or broken. A doctor shows us our physical toxins; God directs us to our spiritual ones.

Jesus implored his disciples to be meek because he didn't want arrogance and self-exaltation to become spiritual toxins to them. He promised that if they were meek, they would inherit the earth.[33] The same applies to us.

What is meant by inheriting the earth? Through Jesus' death and resurrection, he bequeathed to us a legacy to inherit peace and prosperity on earth. But like any gift, we have to make the decision to fully accept it. This inheritance is promised now and for eternity when the eternal kingdom is established on earth. Make no mistake, this does not mean we are promised financial rewards. True peace and prosperity is living a life that reflects the humble faith, truthfulness, and kindness of Jesus. When our character shines with God's abundant grace, we inherit the respect of others who are the benefactors of our meekness.

Kathie Lee described her husband as a humbled man who passed away without regrets. Frank made huge mistakes. But because he believed in self-examination, he humbly asked for forgiveness and accepted the consequences. He experienced huge prosperity in the public's eye. But what he valued the most and what brought him peace in the end was his faith in God, the love of his family, and the respect of those in his profession. He was meek and respected by others, and he inherited peace for eternity.

David was born into a humble beginning. He was barely a teenager, a mere shepherd boy, when he was called upon to defeat Goliath. But he soon discovered that fame was fleeting. He made huge mistakes and attempted to cover them up. The Psalms are plentiful with his self-examination, repentance to God, and willingness to take the consequences for his sins. What David valued the most was his faith in God. He was meek and respected by God, and he inherited peace for eternity.

After a humble start in a reed bassinet, Moses self-examined, questioned and got angry with God, and made mistakes. But he literally inherited the earth by leading his people to the Promised Land, even though he personally didn't step foot in Canaan. He sought to honor God and be faithful to the calling on his life. He knew God would bring his people all the way home. Moses was meek and respected by his people and by God, and he inherited peace for eternity.

In the past when I thought about my early days of being overweight, bullied, taunted, teased, abused, raped, threatened, and told I was a failure, I had little to be proud of. Meekness helped me survive. I wanted to believe in humanity. But at the time, I questioned if anyone could ever be proud of me, especially myself.

It's my contention God allowed the tough times in my life (though he did not cause them) so that when he brought me to the Mrs. America pageant, I could remember my roots and guard my heart against spiritual toxins. In 1996, I competed as Mrs. Minnesota at the Mrs. America pageant in Las Vegas. This formerly overweight, bullied woman was called to do something totally outside her comfort zone and beyond her wildest imagination.

During the intimidating swimsuit competition, the fifty-one contestants stood outside on risers that overlooked the Rocky Mountains. I memorized the panoramic splendor as I indulged in the majesty of the mountains. I fought back the tears and said to myself, "I'm at the *Mrs. America Pageant*!!!" I never wanted to forget the healing God gave me, right there on those risers, even though I felt like a foreigner in a place I never imagined I would visit.

God allowed me to be the last one Dad spoke to before he passed from Alzheimer's. Dad embraced our relationship, and he always knew exactly who I was. He knew I always tried to treat him and others with tenderness, despite my failings. He owned a piece of my soul, and he knew how much I loved him.

A number of loving family members came to support me during competition week, including my parents. Dad took a lot of video footage from his vantage point in the audience during the final competition. After my beautiful friend Cynthia was crowned as Mrs. America, I stayed onstage for a short while to greet people and wipe away my tears. It wasn't until after Dad passed away that I saw the video he took during those post-pageant moments. At one point, he zoomed in as close as he could to capture my tears and his thoughts on tape. When I watched the video tape years later, I cried when I heard Dad's voice captured for eternity:

"Cheryl, honey, don't cry. I love you, and I'm so proud of you."

Oh, how the tears poured out! Dad's voice comforted me all those years later, after he already went home to heaven. Hearing that he was proud of me was salve for my soul. Just as my heavenly Father desires for me, I believe Dad desired my meekness far more than he desired my success. He loved me just as I was. That video is a prized possession and causes my tears to flow. What a priceless gift God gave to me—hearing my dad's voice telling me one more time he loved me unconditionally and recognizing God's admonition to be meek.

If we have gone through much, God asks us to give much. He seeks meek-minded people to be his hands and feet to regift his grace to others. And he promises that if we get consumed by spiritual toxins, he will remind us that all successes and accomplishments belong to him. We only achieve much because he calls and equips us to do much.

Exclusion and Peace

Before I was a teenager, allergies and asthma-like issues often kept me indoors. I was allowed to play in the garage during the summer with my best friend Karen until four o'clock in the afternoon. Then

I was relegated back inside the house to sit on the couch to gaze through the picture window. I watched the sun, clouds, and lucky kids who got to run, laugh, ride bikes, and play ball.

Sometimes the kids used chalk to construct tennis courts, baseball diamonds, or bicycle race courses in our cul-de-sac. It amused me. But I mostly felt secluded and excluded. I was jealous, frustrated, embarrassed, overweight, and mocked. Exclusion didn't bring about a feeling of peace. However, witnessing life through a picture window allowed me to become empathetic to those with Alzheimer's—and their caregivers.

Someone with dementia can feel the same emotions of exclusion—sadness, jealousy, inadequacy, frustration, unworthiness, embarrassment, and loneliness. My mom eventually lost nearly all of her short-term memory and frequently said she was lonely because no one visited, called, or walked the hallways. She couldn't remember sitting for hours with other residents talking about boys, the nurses who brought her medications, the kitchen crew who sought her out and greeted her with smiles, or exercising with other residents in fitness class. She forgot that my husband and I called her twice daily, nor could she recall our Sunday mornings at church together. She often proclaimed in the church hallways that she didn't have any money because I kept it all. A few stares later, I quietly reminded Mom that I was her life manager, and that her money was well-protected and overseen by the courts.

My mom often felt sad and alone, and she even told us she wanted to take drugs to "make her dead." What haunting words coming from my mother's lips! She got frustrated thinking someone had stolen her pens, coffee, toothpaste, or even her dentures. Yet the only thing stolen was her memory.

Those with moderate to severe dementia frequently endure panic attacks because their reality is disjointed, and it becomes difficult for them to get back to a place of peace. Panic attacks appear to occur more frequently in vascular dementia than in Alzheimer's.[34] Unfortunately, my mom suffered with both kinds of dementia and experienced several panic attacks that were exacerbated by her history of anxiety disorder and depression.

Mom exhibited many episodes of confusion and agitation about my dad, forgot his name, believed she recently talked to him, and asked if he was alive. One evening, she dialed 911 and demanded they find her husband and bring her home to Camden, the neighborhood in Minnesota where she spent her childhood and early years of marriage. It was one of these episodes that triggered her first definitive panic attack. Her blood pressure was nearly 200 / 120. As the gentle nurse held her hand while I talked to Mom over the phone, her blood pressure went down.

She didn't know any other number to call, and in her high anxiety, she felt all alone. I didn't have the power to rectify her reality with truth because she couldn't remember the truth. In moments like this when I was powerless to make things better for Mom, I battled the most with sadness, doubts, anger, and selfishness. I just wanted my old life back. I wished there was a way to roll back the fog in Mom and give me back *my* normal.

The emotions of exclusion also manifest regularly in many caregivers, especially for those who care for loved ones with Alzheimer's in their own homes. Caregivers experience emotions of loss (gradual loss of a loved one, finances, or even control of their own lives), loneliness (from isolation), or jealousy that *others* can go to events or vacation. They feel inadequate over failures, sadness because Alzheimer's steals their joy, or embarrassment. There were a number of times when I fought being embarrassed by the actions of my mom when she cussed in church or at other residents in the nursing home. I wanted to run and hide from the disease. Somehow it always found me. What I really wanted to find was peace.

Jesus promises peace, even in the hard trials of caregiving. He made the ultimate sacrifice to restore unity and peace with others, between others, and within ourselves. Our citizenship resides firmly in the body of Christ.

Do you feel excluded or lonely in caregiving? I did, and it's normal. In those times, I dug deep to rebuke the lies that I wasn't good enough or working hard enough, that this was too much for me to handle, or that no one cared about what I was doing. I focused on the fact I was a child of God. Caregiving is one of the toughest tasks a person can choose to do for someone else. Many don't even try.

If God chose you to be a caregiver, you'll be leaving a legacy of love to pass down through future generations. He will give you the fruit of peace to successfully perform this calling on your life. You will experience peace as you pass it on. Sometimes you will need to ask God to boldly show you where you can tangibly witness his peace because sometimes it is tediously hard to find.

You, my friend, are a beloved child of God. You are never alone. He won't ever exclude you from his presence, and his peace will abundantly surround you. I know sometimes you can't feel his peace because the task of caregiving is too overwhelming. You may be on duty twenty-four hours a day, heavily sleep deprived, choosing between your son's championship Little League game or bringing your loved one to the doctor, changing soiled sheets for the third time in a day, or tearfully asking someone for help and being turned down. Again.

Through it all, Jesus never leaves, never fails, and never excludes you from his peace.

Like me, do you find it hard to even imagine how scary it feels for someone with Alzheimer's? Alzheimer's is a progressively thickening fog that never goes away, except for occasional moments of clarity. People with Alzheimer's feel increasingly alone as the memories that once made up their existence can no longer reach the surface.

They get suspicious of others who *must* have stolen something. Alzheimer's doesn't allow them to logically process information—if it's missing, it was stolen. No other reason is possible. The reality is that all of their memories have been stolen. It's difficult for them to live in a world of peace when it feels like their thoughts have declared a mutiny.

But you can be equipped to bring a fragment of serenity into their world. If we obediently live in meekness, we inherit God's presence. When we are filled with God's presence, we are able to bring our loved ones back to a place of peace.

Most of the writing of this manuscript took place while my mom was still alive. It allowed me to learn much about myself, my relationship with God, and my loving responsibility toward my mom. Writing this chapter on meekness and peace empowered me to idle down the throttle of my stress a little bit. I discovered a reservoir of peace upon which to draw and regift to my mom, sometimes with a bounty of humor.

During one of my nightly phone calls, Mom asked me to get her more toothpaste. I knew we just bought some a few weeks earlier, but I told her we could check to see if she truly needed more.

A few days later, after church, I looked in her medicine cabinet as promised. Lo and behold, a totally unused tube of Colgate was on the top shelf. It hadn't even collected dust yet.

"How did that get there?" said my mom.

"Do you have . . . another one?" I said.

Responsive to my question, she quietly escorted me into her bedroom and stopped at her bureau. She docilely opened her underwear drawer. On the left-hand side, lying neatly beside her gently folded underwear and socks, was her nearly used-up tube of toothpaste still housed in its original box. She always kept those stupid boxes, and I giggled to see that some things never changed!

I tried to keep my composure. With a straight face, I looked at her and said, "Um, Mom, do you *always* keep it in there?"

"Yes."

"Mom, do you *want* to keep it in your underwear drawer?"

"Yes."

I replied, "Well, okaaaaaaaaaaay then!"

I walked out of her room with a big grin, praising God for little problems, lots of peace, and Mom's new normal. At least in the underwear drawer, no one would *steal* it!

My caregiving prayer for you is this: God never excludes, no matter who we are or what we've done. He wants us to be free of spiritual toxins and use the gifts and calling he gave us before we were born. My prayer is that even in the toxic moments of caregiving, you can see that He's your number one fan and biggest cheerleader. He never calls without equipping—sometimes it's just hard to see.

~~~~~~~~~~~~~~~~~~

Prayer: Thank you for the promise that, in all circumstances, you draw me closer to you through them. When your Word places a calling on my life, give me the peace, courage, and strength to fulfill it. May those I love always feel secure and at peace, despite the skewed moments of their lives. For the sake of loved ones, may your peace be within them always. In Jesus' name. Amen.[35]

Chapter 5

Ten Minutes of Terror

Blessed are those who hunger and thirst for
righteousness, for they will be filled.

Matthew 5:6

But the fruit of the Spirit is . . . forbearance . . .

Galatians 5:22

"Have a great night's sleep, Mama, and we'll talk tomorrow," I
said, closing out another of our tender evening phone calls
that were always seasoned with whispers of "I love you."

Mom gently hung up the phone and checked the time on the
miniature clock sitting on the worn, fifty-year old table placed next
to her cushioned glider. Precisely eight o'clock and time for bed. She
enjoyed the freedom of living in her senior community apartment,
but she religiously followed the itinerary of her bedtime ritual—
the momentary sanctuary for her mind and soul. Sleep granted
permission for pleasant memories or fantasies to evict the intrusion
of Alzheimer's in her life. As Alzheimer's progresses, peaceful sleep
becomes an oxymoron. Nightmares begin to exclude slumber's

solace, and when awakened into reality, they invite moments fraught with terror.

She slowly stood up from her glider to walk in silence to her bedroom. She gently unlaced and removed her shoes, methodically placing them side by side in the identical location in the closet. After changing into her cotton nightgown and pulling down the comforter on her bed, she paused to think about what came next. She sauntered into the bathroom to take out her teeth and wash her face. She grimaced at the mirror as she eyed yet another new wrinkle, vowing to never use soap again since that's what obviously caused the new and unwanted crevice on her face. She checked the lock on the door for the third time to make sure it was securely fastened, crawled into bed, switched off the light, laid her gray locks onto her pillow, and fell into a profound sleep. Her increased dosage of donepezil provoked an intense night of vivid dreams.

At midnight, the perceived ring of the phone broke the stillness.

"Beverly, dear, we need you as soon as possible. Your father and I need your help. We'll meet you in the parking lot. Please help us right away," said her mother, who had passed away fifteen years earlier.

Mom rushed to get up and help. She was now fully awake, but she was totally unable to comprehend that both her parents were no longer living. Reality eluded her. She slid into her bathrobe and slippers, ran out of her apartment and into the main corridor without her keys, and pressed the down arrow repeatedly as she waited for the elevator to finally take her downstairs. Her heart began beating faster as fear hijacked her peace. She couldn't understand why her parents needed her help. She cussed in frustration until the elevator finally arrived, hustled into its cold chill, and paced in the carriage until its descent to the main floor was complete.

She impatiently stood in front of the elevator door, brusquely demanding it to open. After breaking free from the confines of the elevator, she rushed through the foyer and front door, which locked behind her. The bite of the frosty air and the icy snow offered no deterrent, and she began to scour the parking lot for the familiar black sedan, only to find that her parents were not there. She began shivering, finally beginning to realize that she was outside with no mittens, scarf, or boots, and no keys to get past the locked door.

Terror gripped her. The frightening, vivid nightmare had become her reality. Frustrated and defeated, my mom frantically tried to get back into the building. For more than ten minutes, she pounded and cussed and lamented, extremely agitated because no one would let her in. She couldn't remember that no one was there at night.

"Let me in! Someone let me in here! Open the door right now! I have to get in!" she cried.

She relentlessly tried the security code without success and resigned herself to sleeping in the cold foyer. She tried the code one last time—finally with success. She was exhausted as she journeyed her way back to the warmth of her apartment and the safety of her familiar bed.

Mom told us the next day about having vivid dreams and trying to meet her parents in the parking lot. She feared she was losing her mind. We confirmed her account of this heartbreaking incident by viewing the security video. It exposed her extreme anger, intense fear, sad frustration, and absolute hopelessness. My mom was excluded from her memories, her parents, and her home. We silently welcomed her into the sixth stage of Alzheimer's, hallmarked by wandering, sundowning, and delusions.

Chuck and I were also terrorized by that night. We recognized that change was required in Mom's level of care in order to keep her safe, so we reduced her donepezil and began the process of filing for guardianship.

Another personal story about exclusion will forever live in the heart of my son, Matt. In the eyes of our children, we are superheroes disguised as moms.

I loathe ridiculous things that get in my way of accomplishing a task. Inanimate objects are *not* going to defeat me. Hear me roar!

When I went through a major life change about a decade ago, I got my treasured possessions successfully stuffed into my new home. However, all the little stuff that makes a house functional was still undone, like hooking up the cable television in my bedroom.

Matt became a technology genius by the ripe old age of twelve and was my sole go-to guy to get my cable working. The only thing keeping me from watching *Leave It to Beaver* reruns was a bureau the size and weight of a circus elephant. The bureau was my television stand and had to be moved away from the wall in order to hook up the cable.

Matt and I first tried the counting thing ("one, two, three—*lift!*") a few times. That didn't work. Next, we braced our backs against the wall and tried to push the bureau away with our feet. That didn't work—the circus elephant morphed into a tank.

Seeing my life flash before my eyes and grieving the fact I would *not* have cable that day, I stood up and said, "Child, back away from the wall and no one gets hurt!"

He could only meekly exclaim, "Mom?!"

I repeated, "Back. Away. From. The. Wall. *Now!*"

He hustled in his retreat to the doorway, recognizing that Mama Bear just came out of her den and meant business. Nothing and no one messes with Mama Bear.

I returned to the tank, ready to defeat the enemy, and I took some deep breaths. I braced myself against the wall, leaned over, picked up the corner of the bureau, and moved it eight inches from the wall. All by myself!

Matt's eyes were as big as a super moon. He again exclaimed, this time with confidence, "*MOM!* How did you *do* that?!"

The simple answer was that it just needed to be done. The real answer was that I truly didn't have a clue where that strength came from. I just knew the bureau was not going to defeat me. Under my son's direction, I hooked up the cable and turned on the television. We plopped on the bed, lauded our successes, and watched *Gilligan's Island*.

My son is now an adult and out on his own as an industrial engineer, and we still talk about that bureau. I remind him to never question a mother's love for her children. If he's ever in trouble, he knows I will move heaven and earth (and an oversized bureau) to help him. I will defend those I unconditionally love, and nothing will stop me. My children will never be excluded from my life nor from my heart, no matter how many miles separate us or what I have to move to get there.

Those with severe dementia feel excluded from their very lives! Reality disappears and memories are extinguished. They feel lonely much of the time because they can't remember nor accurately discern how much time has passed since their last visitor arrived. We frequently heard the woe in Mom's voice when she said she was always lonely and no one ever came to see her. It wasn't the truth, but it was her perceived reality. In one day, she could spend hours talking to her lady friends, praying with ladies from church, and playing bingo, only to tell me in the evening phone call that no one ever talked to her. She lived in the terrors of darkness and flagrant lies of exclusion because her memory was relinquished to dementia. Similarly, without Jesus, we live in the blindness and lies of exclusion with a hunger and thirst for a way out of the darkness.

God created Adam and Eve out of darkness and into innocence. He prohibited them from partaking in only one thing from the Garden of Eden, which was the tree of the knowledge of good and evil. They succumbed to the seductive thirst for knowledge, chose to sin against God by eating from the tree, and were ultimately banished from the Garden because of their blatant disobedience. Not only did Adam and Eve lose their residence in the Garden, they lost their innocence. Adam and Eve were exiled from sharing eternity with God because sin cannot coexist in God's presence— only righteousness. This was the original sin and the first separation, and all generations thereafter continue to be born with a desire to fill the natural void in the soul caused by exclusion from God. The good news is that righteousness with God can be regained—but only through the blood of Jesus. Through Christ, undefeated innocence returns.

Some people fill that void through relationships, control, pride, or pursuit of their own personal needs and desires. Others seek to fill it through good deeds and success. Others simply deny its existence. However, exclusion *from* God can only be eternally filled by restoring a righteous relationship *with* God through the blood of Jesus. Jesus was and is the only one on earth to live a life of true righteousness and be free from guilt and sin.[36]

All have sinned and fall short of the glory of God, and it's impossible to be pure from sin—apart from God. Good deeds are not a boarding pass into heaven, because even one sin erases every good deed. Adam and Eve sinned one time and were forever banished from the Garden. Doing good works to win God's favor doesn't work either because past, present, and future sins can never exist in his presence. However, reconciliation with God is possible with grace and justification through the blood of Jesus.[37]

God the Father gave us a grace gift in his Son, Jesus. When my husband offers me an anniversary love gift, it becomes mine only if I accept and open it. If I keep the unopened gift high on a shelf collecting dust, I have rejected it. It never becomes mine. God presents all of us with a gift wrapped up in an eternal bow of salvation. The gift is named Jesus. We can enter into a personal relationship with Jesus because of the gift he gave us all when he hung on the splintered cross. However, if we don't accept and open the gift of Jesus Christ, we reject him and remain excluded from eternity with God.

I reached a point in my life where I desperately wanted redemption. I wanted the void of exclusion to be like my breath on a mirror—quickly gone without a trace. My burden was heavy. My sins were numerous. How could I ever be worthy of a guiltless relationship with Jesus Christ when my life was defined by sin and failure? When I looked in the mirror, all I could see was pain and unworthiness. My life felt out of control and without purpose. I was disgusted with my life. What purpose could this mistake-of-a-life have?

I believed in God most of my life and wanted to believe that what he said in the Bible was true. But it wasn't until April 1984 that I recognized that my life was filled with exclusion and emptiness. I thanked Jesus for bearing my sins on his shoulders and shedding his own blood as his broken body carried what should have been *my* cross. He willingly died for me as payment in full for the price of my sins. His lifeless body was laid to rest in a barren cave, and he awoke from the recesses of death to walk among humanity before ascending to his throne in heaven. I asked for his forgiveness and help to desire righteousness instead of sin. I asked him to be Lord of my life and to show me his purpose and plan for my life.

On that day, I was forgiven. My sins were paid in full! My innocence before God was restored because it was no longer defeated by sin. Without his mercy, I don't know how I could have helped my mom not feel the exclusion in her damaged world if there were still lonely barriers in my own.

I still make mistakes and still sin, but my desire is to follow God's leading *in* my life and his direction *for* my life. Step by step, he heals my internal scabs. But the scars remain as a reminder that he brought restoration and the promise of eternal life into my life through his righteousness, and I will never again be excluded from God's presence.

Life on this side of heaven is never perfect. Concerns and opposition routinely surface. I have times of tremendous sadness, especially since losing my mom. But Christ truly does lead me through it all in his timing, not mine. He rejoices with me through every storm and every success. And through his help, the joys outweigh the pain.

God doesn't cause hardships, but he can allow them in our lives when it suits his purposes. God doesn't cause Alzheimer's, but through it he teaches me perseverance, patience, and compassion.

We are never promised a pain-free life when we have a relationship with Jesus; rather, we are promised he will never leave nor forsake us. We can call on him anytime, day or night. The more time we spend in his presence, the more we will experience his power and authority.

God can be trusted with the details of whatever you're facing. He is who he says he is, and is ready to shepherd your journey. More than thirty years ago, I prayed:

> Father God, I know I am a sinner and fall short of righteousness. I don't want to be excluded from your promise of restoration and eternal life. I make mistakes and sin, but my desire is to follow your leading and direction for my life. There is emptiness in my life without you. Jesus died in my place and rose again so I could spend eternity with you. Please forgive my sins yesterday, today, and tomorrow. Jesus, please come into my life as my Lord and Savior, fill me with your presence, and guide my life through the wisdom of the Holy Spirit. In the name of Jesus, I pray. Amen.

I was no longer excluded or alone. Jesus Christ filled the hole in my soul, and I was guaranteed eternity in heaven with God. My spiritual hunger—that void first created in the Garden of Eden when Adam and Eve were separated from God—was eternally satisfied, and my sin debt was paid in full by the righteousness of Jesus.

I understood the meaning of Revelations 3:20 that Jesus stood knocking at the door of my life. If I opened the door and invited him in, he promised to come in. When I prayed that prayer thirty years ago, I heard him knocking, opened the door, and invited him into my life. That included my life with Alzheimer's.

My husband and I were in constant contact with Mom through our daily phone calls, and we saw her at least once a week. The nursing staff knew us by name, and they recognized how involved we were with her life. Even though we didn't provide care for her in our home, we were her legal guardians and made all of her life decisions.

Some days she got set off because she didn't have any white bread or couldn't remember where she left her purse. Other days she was frustrated because she couldn't get her key in the mailbox, didn't know what day it was, or why she heard noises or voices outside her door. Many days offered a repeat of the day before. The movie *Groundhog Day* became a montage of my life. In that movie, the same twenty-four-hour period kept replaying over and over. How reassuring it was to know I could get my feet back on the trail God laid out for me, rise in the middle of the night to thank him, and even when there appeared to be no way out from the frustrations, remember his plans for me (not to harm, but to give hope and a future[38])!

I am now of the age where my sleep consists of covers on, covers off, covers on, covers off. Brief interludes of tropical heat frequently come around three o'clock in the morning. When we moved to Arkansas and away from our adult children, God lovingly showed me that the greatest influence I could have on our children was to be a prayer warrior for them. Three o'clock became my morning prayer time to thank him, to seek protection over our family and specifically each child, and to ask for wisdom in helping Mom. My hot-flash prayers changed from a time of deprivation to a time of residing in the presence of my Abba Father. The more I resided in his presence, the more I learned how to pray, receive answers, and walk in his will for my life.

Because Jesus paid our debt in full, we are promised to be filled with his presence. We can't be assured the road will be easy, but we can be guaranteed that the Holy Spirit will guide us through each circumstance from beginning to end with hope and a future—even when it seems like life continually presses the repeat button.

Patience? I don't have time for patience!

When we turn to Jesus to fill the void of exclusion with his gift of salvation, we are defined by a new perspective and live our lives through the lens of his Word instead of the lens of the world. That new lens is the fruit of the Spirit, which includes the gift of forbearance.

Forbearance is defined as displaying self-control or patience with difficult people or in difficult situations without anger or fear, or offering mercy instead of enforcement of a debt that is due. Jesus is the ultimate forbearer because he offers each of us mercy instead of death, and no one will ever exceed his relentless patience.

Praying for patience has always been tough for me because I know that the lessons required to learn it can be extraordinarily painful. We learn the most about God and his desires for our lives in the valleys of life, not through the mountaintop experiences.

I certainly did not exhibit a great deal of patience when I tried to move my mountain of a bureau to get cable television. I placed both my son and myself in a situation where we could have been physically hurt. It would have been a better choice if I waited for my older son to get home; together, the three of us could have gotten the job done quickly and without risk. However, I didn't want to wait and refused to be defeated by an inanimate object the size of a hippo. Forbearance? Not me. Granted, I did move the mountain, no one was hurt, and the television worked. And Matt learned I will always fight for him and never exclude him from my life. However, it would have been preeminently valuable if I used the experience to demonstrate a life lesson about waiting on God, praising in all situations, and embracing the virtue of patience.

Romans 5:3–4 suggests how troubles promote *passionate patience* in us and forge *the tempered steel of virtue.*[39] What a powerful, life-changing word picture.

Tempering happens when alloys are heat-treated to increase toughness by decreasing hardness. Believing the grace is greener on

God's side, I need to embrace the tough situations that can develop a passionate patience in me—resulting in greater toughness (flexibility, strength, and durability) and less hardness (harshness and rigidity) of my moral character. In other words, patience breeds resiliency.

As a caregiver, I wanted to show Mom patience and flexibility from the harsh realities of what her life became through Alzheimer's. I desired to give her a peaceful quality of life.

I have communicated with many others who struggle with caring for loved ones with dementia. It's easy to *say* we love the person and hate the disease (have you found yourself saying that yet?). But it was still incredibly difficult to hold back my impatience when I explained to Mom for the umpteenth time she was not living in a campground, a motor home, or a hotel, or I tried to rationalize with her that her phone cord couldn't reach that far if her room was on wheels. Her typical response was, "Well, okay-*eeeee*"—the response that sounds like, "Well I still don't believe you, but, well, what*ever!*"

It was also hard to be patient when Mom yelled at me when she was certain I took her coat and purposely shrunk it so it wouldn't fit her anymore. Passionate patience reminded me to not simply tell her she was gaining weight, but rather to redirect her attention until I could get that shrunken coat safely back into the confines of her closet!

When Alzheimer's began its assault on disconnecting my mom from me, it grew unpleasant for me to hear her repetitive questions about *her daughters*. She loved us dearly, desperately wanted to find us, and called me in hopes that I could help her find them. Each time she called, I answered, "Hi, Mom" (with an emphasis on *Mom*). During a number of those calls, she immediately started asking if I knew where her daughters were because Dad was going to pick them up and bring them to see her. I explained I *was* her daughter, to which she replied she meant her *young* daughters. I then explained I *was* her youngest daughter, and I was over fifty-five years old. She would then start over from the beginning. Sound exhausting? It was, and I waged war against my tears. But those trials taught me to be more passionately patient and resilient. How could I point my mom to Jesus if she couldn't even see my compass in my own agitation?

Are you caring for someone at home around the clock? If so, your situation is much tougher because it places more demands on you and your family. But forbearance is still a gift given to you directly from God. He's available 24/7 to lead you to the path of passionate patience and making it through the next thirty seconds. I learned valuable lessons about tempering patience, rather than displaying my impatient temper.[40]

I tried to convince myself, sometimes reluctantly, that deep down in the depths of my mom's brain she knew I was doing the best I could and was grateful for that. I constantly reminded myself that she lived one or more decades in the past and related to me from a former decade. Through it all, I could be her ray of hope and encouragement.

Alzheimer's stage six brought my mom back to her teenage years and early days of marriage. When she told me how perfect my dad was and how they never fought, I thought about how grateful I was for her loss of the painful memories of their hard times together. When she asked me who was taking care of her daughters, I chose to laugh at the humor of wishing I was four decades younger and still needed my parents to care for me.

Passionate patience was a requirement when I assisted my mom back to a place of peace during her panic attacks. If she sensed a tsunami in my emotions, I would be incapable of helping her find calm in her own storm. She trusted me to help her. Through passionate patience and forbearance, she could release her fears more quickly. Sometimes she needed a medication assist from a nurse. But she did best when the grace gift of passionate peace was regifted to her through God's presence in me.

I tried to stay grounded by believing in my personal relationship with Jesus. He experienced great trials, tribulations, and sorrow long before I was even born. I am never excluded from his presence. I talked with Mom about the hope we have in Jesus, which brought her moments of peace. We prayed the Lord's Prayer together daily. And I was gently reminded to be patient and longsuffering with my mom because her burdens were far greater than mine.

My caregiving prayer for you is this: Others graciously offered the advice that I needed to dig deeper within myself. That only made things more difficult because I was a weak vessel with a fractured emotional core. Mom's Alzheimer's wasn't a moral or emotional problem in me. It was a disease that was stealing our memories and our time together. By grace I learned if I hungered and thirsted for righteousness through Christ above all else, he would show me how to be passionately patient with greater flexibility and less harshness, both to my mom and to myself. When you're confronted with a behemoth (like my bureau), my prayer is that Christ alone assists you in moving it out of the way and guides you to a place of safety.

~~~~~~~~~~~~~~~

Prayer: I desire to praise and be a blessing to you every day, Lord. You are who you say you are, and you deserve my praise. Show me how to dwell in your righteousness. You are kind, merciful, slow to anger, fair, and filled with love. You showcase your compassion to me. Thank you for lifting me up from underneath the loads I carry. I praise your name forever and ever. In Jesus' name. Amen.[41]

Chapter 6

Nothing Says Love
Like Bubble Wrap

Blessed are the merciful, for they will be shown mercy.

Matthew 5:7

But the fruit of the Spirit is . . . kindness . . .

Galatians 5:22

A ministry name eluded me for months. Every time I came up with *the* perfect name, I discovered someone else was already using it. Trusting God to provide the name was the obvious preference, but somehow I must not have been receiving his emails. It seemed to me like it was taking forever. I ultimately knew that when he did nudge me with *his* title, no one else would have ever used it.

I began discussions with one of our pastors about growing this ministry into a Bible study in our church. One Sunday morning before church, Pastor Kevin told me to give him a synopsis and a title. My excitement plummeted as I explained to him I had struggled with a title for a long time and was always coming up empty. I promised to do my best. Emotionally I felt slightly defeated, but rushing God is never a beneficial option. "God is never late, never early, and always on time" rang in my ears.

That same morning, only a few minutes after my chat with Pastor Kevin, the worship service began, and every congregational song related to grace. *Grace.* Hmm. The sweet sound of that amazing word resonated in me, and my spirit was replete with joy. But what word could I put with *grace?* A two-word descriptive title would be perfect. I continued to sing the worship songs about abundant grace while filled with the distraction of seeking God's revelation—on my timing, of course.

We sat down for the offering, and the choir started singing as the tithes were collected. I began writing notes until I could no longer see through my tears. The choir sang about grace! I experienced a moment in the presence of my heavenly Father, and he gave me the name I sought. I thought about how God fills us with his abundant grace in order to share it with others. I thought about birthday and Christmas gifts. I'm embarrassed to tell you that, with an ounce of hilarity, a picture of *white elephant* Christmas gifts came to my mind—those obtuse gifts we *regift* to someone else.

Wait! That was it! *Regifted Grace* is the pinnacle of God's abundant grace poured out on us so we can regift it to others—what an amazing expression of God's love passing through us to our loved ones with Alzheimer's! We are imperfect vessels, but he compassionately gives us his perfect gift of grace and delights in us when we regift it to others.

I knew I would never forget what God whispered in my soul, but I wrote down the name and couldn't wait to get home, do the research, and make sure no one else was using it. I knew such a beautiful title belonged to God, and he had reserved it for this ministry. I gave it back to the Lord and felt a great peace as our senior pastor approached the platform to start his sermon. I glanced up at the big screens in front of the worship center and noted the title of Pastor Tad's sermon. Can you guess? The title, in bold letters that were taller than my bedroom bureau, was *Grace*. God revealed it for a third time, just to make sure I wouldn't miss it. I had impatiently waited on God's timing for months. In one morning, three times, he revealed it to me—God dispatched *Regifted Grace*.

That's what God's grace is all about. It's always in his hands, power, and authority. It's never late, never early, and always on time. Grace is undeserved and unmerited, a divine favor from God for a sacred purpose or for spiritual renewal and growth. He freely gives it, just as he freely gave his Son as a love sacrifice for sin. We are truly saved by grace![42]

There is absolutely nothing we can do to earn God's grace except to put him first in our lives through a relationship with Jesus. We can neither ask for grace nor expect it. It is always at the Father's discretion. And so is his mercy.

God's counterpart to grace (being given something wonderful that we *don't* deserve) is mercy (not being given the consequences we *do* deserve). Mercy substitutes a consequence with compassion and kindness. God is the eternal Judge, and mercy is his absolution for our iniquities. God offers us eternal life, even though we deserve eternal death on a cross. By mercy and grace, God pardons our sins through Jesus and pours out his love into our lives. Before we can *regift* grace, we must first *receive* it through Jesus Christ. Grace can't flow *through* us until it is filled *in* us by the presence of the Holy Spirit.

In previous chapters, I discussed exclusion as being a hardship, particularly to those with dementia who can feel excluded from their own lives because memories of their lives become nonexistent. However, by God's grace and mercy, we can never be excluded or separated from the love of God. Jesus knows what it feels like to experience the darkest hours, because he experienced them first. Through him, we are promised that neither death nor life, neither present nor future, nor anything in creation can separate us from the love of God and his gifts of grace and mercy.[43]

God doesn't cause sadness, pain, or Alzheimer's. But he can choose to allow it in our lives if it serves an eternal purpose. I don't ever deserve a painless and tear-free life. In fact, he tells us, "...for our light and momentary troubles are achieving for us an eternal glory that far outweighs them all."[44] On this side of heaven, I won't have an adequate answer as to how Alzheimer's could ever serve an eternal purpose. However, I do know that I am a better woman, daughter, wife, sister, friend, and mother because of it. God gave me the strength to step over betrayals and persecution. He healed and forgave. He allowed me to lean into Jesus and learn about compassion and sacrifice. I was used by God to nurture a loved one who was in great fear of the disease that robbed her of priceless memories. I was called to regift God's grace to my life's best friend—my mom.

Sometimes there are consequences for our actions, and we get what we deserve. If I consumed four decadent, irresistible scoops of chocolate ice cream topped with chocolate fudge and whipped cream every day for a year without increasing my exercise, I deserve the possible end results—excess weight, diabetes, or even Alzheimer's. However, if I chose a whole-foods diet, replete of gluten, dairy, eggs, and sugar, I still could end up with heart disease, cancer, or even Alzheimer's, even though in my mind I didn't deserve it. The point is that sometimes bad things just happen. Alzheimer's doesn't discriminate—five million Americans of all ethnic backgrounds, family history, and health matrices have it.

When Jesus was hung on the cross, two convicted criminals were being crucified alongside him. One criminal mocked Jesus by saying, "So you're Jesus the Christ, Savior of the world? Let's see you prove it. I bet you can't save yourself, or us for that matter. Show us who you *really* are!"

The second criminal responded, "Do you think that's going to help us? We're guilty as sin, but this man next to us never did anything wrong. We deserve to die, but not this man. Jesus, please don't forget me."

Jesus replied to him, "I won't forget you. I promise. You will join me in heaven today."

As Jesus hung on the cross and prepared to die, he suffered excruciating and unimaginable torture, which he did not deserve. Greater than the pain he felt was the joy he experienced giving the gift of eternal life in order for us to serve God. As a caregiver, greater than the pain I felt was the joy I experienced by serving my mom and interceding on her behalf. I could be angry at the disease and question what she did to deserve it, or wonder what my father did to deserve it. But the reality is that I was chosen to serve them for the glory of God. My parents' and my final destinations are heaven with Jesus—that's his solemn promise.

There is a tightly connected, closed support group on social media of over four thousand people from around the world who are involved in caring for someone with dementia. A common thread among many of the caregivers is their loneliness and overwhelming desire to give up. But when the journey is over and the dust settles, a majority of caregivers are grateful they made the agonizing sacrifices in exchange for the special and unique time with their loved ones. Many of us expressed that we would have done nearly anything to have one more day, but still the joy of caregiving was far greater than the anguish.

It was agonizing to watch my dad slip away, and it was an arduous task to be a daily eyewitness to my mom slipping further away. She eventually forgot most of the people and places that were once important in her life. With God's help, I was allowed to delicately hold her in my heart and in my arms, and she remembered me to the very end.

The love of my parents is far greater than any sacrifice on my part. That's what I will choose to carry me through to the end of my days on earth. With God's promises of grace and mercy, and his further promise that nothing will separate me from his presence, he armed me with fearless courage to make it through the next minutes, hours, days, and months until Mom and I said goodbye until we meet again in heaven.

Jesus taught that those who are merciful and treat people with kindness, forgiveness, gentleness, and compassion are blessed. Mercy is not cruel or harsh. It focuses on others rather than self and offers relief from hardship and suffering. Being merciful is not only an action, it is also a condition of the heart.

Prior to his conversion, Saul (later renamed Paul after his conversion) was a vocal antagonist against the followers of Jesus and passionately desired to place into chains everyone professing to follow him. He asked the high priest to issue arrest warrants in order to threaten the Christians with imprisonment and death. With warrants in hand, Saul and several others headed for Damascus to round up the renegade Christ followers. On their journey, God flashed down a bright light from heaven that propelled Saul to the ground and blinded him. Jesus called out to Saul, "Why do you persecute Me?"

The men traveling with Saul heard the unrecognizable sound of Jesus' voice, but they didn't see anyone. They took Saul by the hand, compassionately guided him down the road to Damascus, and went without food or water for three days.

Meanwhile, in a dream, the Lord instructed a believer named Ananias to place hands on Saul to restore his vision when he arrived in Damascus. At the same time, in a dream, the Lord revealed to Saul that a man named Ananias would restore his sight. Ananias was fearfully resistant, telling the Lord that Saul was arresting all believers. The Lord consoled Ananias, telling him that Saul was chosen to proclaim his name to the Gentiles and that God himself would handle any punishment due to Saul.

When Saul reached Damascus, Ananias told him, "Brother Saul, the Lord Jesus, who appeared to you on the road as you were coming here, has sent me so that you may see again and be filled with the Holy Spirit."[45] Ananias laid hands on Saul, the scales immediately fell from his eyes, and he was given a new name—Paul of Tarsus. He was healed from his physical and spiritual blindness, baptized, and began preaching that Jesus was the Son of God.

What incredible mercy Ananias and Jesus showed Paul! But the story doesn't end there.

As a Christ follower, Paul began to preach about Jesus, much to the chagrin of the Jews who conspired to kill Paul. Paul's followers helped him escape the city to go to Jerusalem. When he arrived, Paul asked to join the apostles. But they were suspicious of his motivations and refused to see him. Barnabas chose to set aside his own fears and personally took Paul to the other apostles to explain that the Lord spoke to Paul on the Damascus road and chose him to fearlessly preach the love of Jesus.

Barnabas was likely one of the early targets of Paul's arrest warrants. Yet, like Ananias, he chose to be merciful to Paul because he recognized God's greater plan. Rather than focusing on themselves, Barnabas and Ananias offered themselves as mentors to Paul through kindness, forgiveness, and compassion, and they gave him relief from his suffering. Even though Paul deserved their punishment, they chose to show mercy, and many people became followers of Christ because Barnabas and Ananias mentored Paul.

Jesus taught by example. He said, "Blessed are the merciful," and gave us a great example through Barnabas and Ananias. They trusted in God's plan and showed mercy to Paul, despite opposition. Many caregivers are called upon to speak up against those who call our loved ones "crazies" or "loonies." Some may think it's funny, but it is not. It is disrespectful and hateful. Barnabas and Ananias showed mercy in defending Paul, and we as caregivers choose to show mercy in defending those who can't defend themselves, especially those with Alzheimer's.

Alzheimer's is a cruel disease. It not only robs people of their present and future, but also robs them of their past, slowly at first, and voraciously in the final stages. Our loved ones seem to age in reverse—caring for them in the end stages becomes more like caring for toddlers.

It was hard to put Dad in a nursing home and explain to him why he needed to wear a clothes protector. On my final day with him, it was emotionally draining to feed him one spoonful at a time and remind him to swallow. But I chose to be blessed, instead of deeply saddened. I got to be the last familiar person to show him compassion, mercy, and grace before he entered his eternal home.

God allowed me to be merciful to Dad, despite my agony over his inability to lift his head right away to greet me or offer me the bear hugs he gave me my whole life. He could barely even eat, and I got to help him. I was allowed to show him selflessness. It wasn't about what he couldn't give me; it was all about the condition of my heart and how I was given one last opportunity to show him one final measure of my love for him.

God was merciful to me when my dad came out of the fog, lifted his head, and said a flamboyant, "Hi!" I didn't get a final bear hug, but as Dad gently squeezed my hand, his eyes radiantly focused on me because he knew who I was.

I'm not sure to whom God was most merciful that final day—Dad, for allowing him to come out of the fog one last time, or me, for allowing a final, special moment with my dad. We were both richly blessed. I blessed Dad, Dad blessed me, and God blessed us both. For the rest of my life, I will carry those blessings with me because I will remember that day as a reflection of God's promise to never abandon us, not even on the doorstep of death.[46]

Jesus asks us to be merciful because mercy is the presence of God in us. God promises never to abandon us or be separated from us, whether in joy or in sorrow. Have you ever wanted to give up because it is so difficult? I tried my best to give everything I could, but Mom still got agitated and aggressive. I never gave up on Mom, but I sure wanted to give up on *it* sometimes—this disease that sucks the life out of its innocent victims. God promises to give us what we need. We call on him, and he will answer and give us strength.

As God is merciful, so are we to be merciful. That's authentic faith! When we open our arms out to Jesus, he shows us kindness, forgiveness, compassion, and relief from suffering as a sacrificial love offering to us. When we open our arms out to someone with Alzheimer's, we show them kindness, forgiveness, compassion, and relief from suffering as a sacrificial love offering to them.[47]

Jesus told his disciples that blessed are the merciful for they will be shown mercy. Conversely, the book of James says God will withhold his mercy and render his judgment upon us if we don't show mercy to others ("what goes around, comes around").

In Matthew 18:23–35, we are told the parable of two bankrupt debtors. The king wanted to settle up debts with his servants. A first servant owed a large sum to the king and couldn't repay him. The king threatened to sell him, his family, and all their possessions. The servant pleaded with the king to have patience with him. The king granted him mercy and forgave his debt.

The first servant then went out and found a second servant who owed *him* money. However, when the second servant pleaded with him for patience, the first servant showed him no mercy and had him thrown into jail. Other servants overheard this and went to the king. The king was outraged with the first servant, rendered his judgment upon the servant, and mandated torture until he could pay off his entire debt. Jesus' teaching is clear—we will be blessed if we are merciful. Conversely, if we don't show forgiveness and mercy when someone asks it from us, God will likewise withhold his mercy from us.

In our final moments together, when I reassured Dad that I would always take care of Mom, I knew it could be a great undertaking and probably the hardest one of my life. At the time, I hadn't given myself permission to see that *it* was already encroaching my mom. But I knew my parents deserved mercy from me because they showed me much mercy during my life. I also knew that God shows his compassionate mercy on me, and when much is given, much is expected. I didn't want to be like the first servant who spit in the face of mercy and was severely punished.

He promises to supply our needs through his presence in our lives. He doesn't expect perfection, but he does reward desire and action with his grace and mercy.

Isn't it fitting that the fruit of kindness can be simply defined as grace and mercy? It can also be described as a gentle nature and a desire to bring peace of mind to others. Kindness is unselfish benevolence. Kindness and mercy are a perfect fit in caregiving. Our loved ones deserve kindness, mercy, and compassion *from* us, and we covet God's grace and mercy *to* us.

It may be difficult to be kind when we are exhausted from multitasking our entire lives in concert with the life of someone else. It might be hard to be kind when we call out for help from others and get only excuses in return. We can be sleep deprived and financially strapped. However, we can thrive in troubled times when we trust God for the outcome. Jesus said, "Don't let your hearts be troubled. Trust in God, and trust in Me."[48] God promised that if we trust him and show mercy and kindness to others, he will bestow mercy and grace on us.

As my parents drifted further into the late stages of Alzheimer's, they became more like little children with each decade of memories lost. They needed help with eating, walking, and personal hygiene. They braved panic attacks and threw temper tantrums. I talked to them softly with simple words, childproofed their rooms, and handled their financial, medical, and legal matters. It was sometimes easy to lose patience with them. I tried to remember to trust that God did indeed have a purpose and a plan for my life and my circumstances.

Sometimes I couldn't decipher fact from fiction in Mom's distorted version of reality. While she was still in assisted living, I started wondering if Mom washed her hair anymore. It started looking limp and oily and didn't have the pretty smell it used to have. I asked her if she showered. She always said, "Yes." I asked her if she used soap. She always said, "Yes."

I placed a freshly opened bar of gentle soap (with a nice little engraving of a bird on it) in her shower. There it stayed, in perfect form, for several months. When she again said she showered *and* used soap, I wanted to strap a single light bulb to the ceiling and interrogate her with a lie detector test until the truth came out. I quickly realized that *the* truth might not be *her* truth. *Her* truth was distorted and no longer reliable. And I also realized that trying to be her parent and catch her in her lies was not a compassionate way to show mercy and grace.

We mentioned it to one of the nurses. She told us that as people age, they don't like to shower because they don't like to get their faces wet. The facility then offered to assist Mom in taking baths twice a week in a wonderful Jacuzzi tub. I was deeply concerned about getting major resistance from my mom, but she absolutely loved it! Soap and all! While the solution met the need, it was painful to watch my mom continue to become more like a child.

Jesus has a special affinity for children, the sick, the poor, and widows. He instructs us to not hinder their ability to be held in his arms. We can lead our loved ones to Jesus by our acts of kindness, or we can hinder them by our acts of selfishness. Kindness is simply showing up, paying bills, making meals, calling, visiting, managing doctor appointments, holding hands, running errands, and placing someone else's needs above our own.

Do you struggle sometimes because it seems like no one sees all that you do for someone else? God sees your kindness through your sacrifices, your physical weakness, your financial struggle, and the days when twenty-four hours are just not enough. He sees your deep compassion because he has deep compassion for you. He knows how hard you are trying to "do it all." And in the end, he will tell you that you have been a good and faithful servant.

You see, the truth is that God is witness to the mercy you are showing in caregiving. He might be the only one. If you are merciful, he will show you mercy—but maybe not right away or in the way you thought he would. I learned that the more time I spent in prayer with him, even in stolen moments during the chores of my day, the more he could illuminate his compassion so I wouldn't miss it.

However and whenever he responds, God's promises are real. Perhaps his mercy won't be manifested until your loved one passes away and you're able to step aside and recognize the richness of the time he gave you with your loved one. After my final goodbye, I could clearly see the abundant blessing in having shared my life with Mom in her final three years—and how I would do it all over again, including all of the struggles.

True kindness is never superficial; it runs deep in a person's core values. It is loving, patient, humble, honoring, not easily angered, enduring, protective, trusting, and unfailing. Kindness is doing for others what you would want others to do for you. Carrying the gift of kindness is much lighter than carrying the weight of frustration and burden.

I recently saw a short video on social media that made me laugh and cry.

My engineer son Matt has always loved bubble wrap. In fact, when he turned eighteen years old, we wrapped all of his gifts in bubble wrap—*pink* bubble wrap. His love for popping bubble wrap started before he could walk. When he was older, he methodically popped each air pocket individually (a first sign of his acumen toward being an engineer), or rolled it up and jumped on all of it at the same time. We took extreme delight in watching him "do his thing" with bubble wrap. Many of his gifts over the years included some component of bubble wrap.

The short social media video showed a daughter caring for her father. He was in late-stage Alzheimer's and could no longer remember her name. He used to be an engineer and believed he could still be one.

The daughter astutely recognized that he needed a job, and the video showed her supervising his task. The tool of his job was a pair of black leather gloves, and his task was to pop bubble wrap. It didn't matter how he did it, he just needed to wear the gloves and pop all the bubbles on individual panels of wrap. He took great pleasure in his work because he regained his importance. The man's daughter checked his work after each perfectly popped panel, reminded him he was getting paid five dollars per panel, and asked if he wanted to do more. He started to remove his gloves, indicating he was done. Through the whole purposeful popping process, the daughter encouraged her father with compassion and large smiles. Her act of kindness, without judgment, allowed him to rediscover a sense of accomplishment. I was moved by her kindness, but I laughed hysterically thinking about perfectly popped pink panels of bubble wrap.

After watching that video, I tried to discover ways to offer Mom a sense of purpose and let her know that she mattered in my life, even if she couldn't always remember I was her daughter.

During our second Christmas season in Arkansas, we asked my mom to help us decorate the Christmas tree with the family heirloom Christmas ornaments that are even older than me—and equally as brittle. Her eyes sparkled as she slowly remembered and handled each of the vintage ornaments, searching the tree for the perfect spot on which to hang each one. She was able to relive some unfaded memories. She was so appreciative of our kindness, and I will always remember that special Christmas. It was a gift for all of us.

Holidays and birthdays became different. The disease changed how I experienced life. I creatively offered acts of kindness and compassion to my mom by finding jobs for her—whether it was hanging antique ornaments on a tree, sorting socks, or pressing cookie cutters into gingerbread dough.[49]

That's what *Regifted Grace* is all about. It's accepting the grace and mercy that God lavishes on us and sharing it as love, joy, kindness, and compassion to those we love, even if they don't know who we are anymore.

My caregiving prayer for you is this: Once I understood that God's mercy and grace to me is intended to then flow through me to Mom, I had a deeper sense of purpose—God's purpose. Every compassionate gift of mercy that you show your loved one truly matters, to your loved one and to God. My prayer is that, going forward, this will make the difficult times a little easier to bear and the tender times even more memorable.

~~~~~~~~~~~~~~~~~~~~~

Prayer: Show me your mercy, Lord, for my eyes cry with sorrow, and my soul is grieving.[50] Show me your mercy, Lord, for life feels fragile.[51] Show me your mercy, Lord; may your love and faithfulness protect me.[52] Show me your mercy, Lord, for you provide a place of sanctuary. I will take refuge in the shadow of your wings until this storm has passed.[53] I love you, Lord. In Jesus' name. Amen.

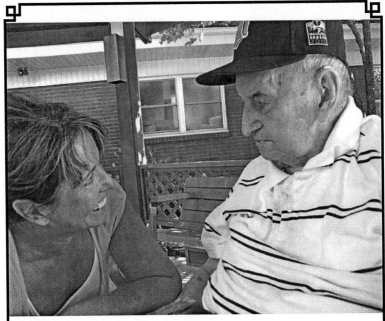

I treasure my final moment with Dad (2010).

Mom escorts me on my wedding day (2009).
Copyright 2009 Picture Place and Barry Howell, Photographer

Dad and Mom always enjoyed being together.

Dad and Mom created adventures together.

Mom loved being a teenager.

Dad's parents, Frank and Mabel, were very proud of his service.

If a guitar was nearby, it was always in Dad's hands.

Dad enjoyed the company of his two favorite
ladies—his wife and his mom.

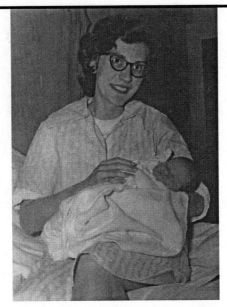

Mom was the first one to hold me, and
I was the last one to hold her.

Mom always liked to drive "fast" cars.

This is one of my treasured photos—
me, Dad, sister Lori, and Mom

My sister Lori and I love to walk through life together

Dad and Mom were all dressed up on their tenth anniversary.

Mom and my husband often relaxed at her
favorite spot—the front porch bench.

Lori and I loved to love Mom.

Chapter 7

Unwavering Sacrifice

Blessed are the pure in heart, for they will see God.

Matthew 5:8

But the fruit of the Spirit is . . . goodness . . .

Galatians 5:22

Dad frequently wore his army fatigue cap and shirt when he puttered around the house, painted, or mowed. They were his favorite work clothes. His baby-blue eyes sparkled from underneath the brim of the green cap, and his effervescent smile brought tender warmth to my soul. When I was a child, I was well aware he was a soldier in the army. But since most of my friends' fathers had also served in the military, it seemed to me, well, *normal*. I took notice of Dad's smile, but I didn't make note of the significance of what he wore. To me, they were just work clothes. Dad served in the Korean War, but he never wanted to talk about it.

My husband and I visited Thomas Jefferson's Monticello in Charlottesville, Virginia, on a brisk afternoon several years after my dad passed away. We met an elderly gentleman named Don who proudly wore his Korean War veteran's cap. As he rested on a bench, I asked him if he served in Korea. He smiled kindly as he tenderly accepted my handshake. I thanked him for his military service and added that my dad also fought in Korea. I asked Don if he talked much about serving in Korea. With tears in his eyes, he shook his head and said he did not. He asked if my dad was still alive. Once again I saw Don's tears as I told him Dad passed away from Alzheimer's. Despite the fact that they never met, I sensed a true camaraderie between Don and my dad.

My husband's cousin also fought in the Korean War and prefers not to talk about it, just like Don and my dad. Silence appears to be a common thread among Korean War veterans, perhaps because that war was often called the Forgotten War. It was wedged between World War II and the Vietnam War, and the troops were dramatically unprepared and depleted after World War II. As a result, the three-year Korean War resulted in over thirty-six thousand American casualties and 104,000 Americans wounded—young men who gave their lives as a sacrifice for freedom.

One of the plaques at the Arkansas Korean War Memorial in Little Rock reads, "The beginning of courage is fear. Every soldier feels it. Bravery is not the lack of fear, but the ability to overcome it and do your duty." The sacrifices of a caregiver are not without fear. But courage begins with fear, and courage breeds bravery and an ability to overcome the fear. You are a brave soldier doing battle caring for someone else. Thank you for giving your life as a living sacrifice for another.

After my dad passed away, I sifted through his personal belongings. I took a deep interest in reading through his discharge papers and the program books from the Korean War reunions he attended. I discovered Dad served in two military campaigns and was given a Korean Service Medal with two bronze service stars. He also received a United Nations Service Medal.

Over five million American troops led the United Nations' forces in Korea. Dad's battalion of the 7th Infantry Division served as a backup position to the front line. Dad was a light weapons infantryman and truck driver. According to what I read, the front line got ambushed, and Dad's line appears to have been called to rescue the injured. I can only imagine Dad's fear. He was a young man of twenty-three years, serving a nation half a world away, and going to the front line of battle where many were injured and dying. I want to believe that his sacrificial bravery overcame his fear.

During the same trip to Charlottesville, my husband and I visited the Korean War Memorial in Washington, D.C., dedicated in 1995 and not yet bearing the names of those who paid the ultimate sacrifice. We strolled down the National Mall toward the Lincoln Memorial. My heart beat erratically as I saw from a distance the nineteen stainless-steel statues, glistening in the cool October sun. The statues depict an advance party of soldiers representing each of the military branches, standing in juniper bushes, separated by granite strips symbolizing the rice paddies of Korea. Each soldier is wearing a poncho covering their weapons and equipment.[54] Their faces hold the exhaustive terror that leached into their souls. These men, like my dad, were younger than the current age of my sons! I ran ahead of my husband, weaving around the other tourists, unable to control my tears as they began to moisten the sidewalk. I unsuccessfully tried to hide my face from the other silent strangers.

A chill went through me as I could literally see my father's face in each of those nineteen statues. I grappled with the emotion he must have felt as he trudged through the rice paddies in the evil bitterness of winter, protected only by his rifle and communications equipment. I empathized with how he dug deep within himself to find the bravery that overcomes fear. I understood why men like Dad and Don were reticent about talking about a war where so many died from enemy acts of aggression. These young soldiers were witness to thousands of orphaned children and encountered a lifetime of death.

I have a deeper respect for my dad after visiting this memorial. I felt his presence within me, and for the first time, I no longer took for granted his sacrifice in the Forgotten War. Dad offered himself as a living sacrifice so others could be free. The huge, granite mural at the National Memorial reminds us that "Freedom Is Not Free."

Twenty years ago, I adopted Romans 12:1–2 as my life verses to represent my spiritual mission statement: "Therefore, I urge you, brothers and sisters, in view of God's mercy, to offer your bodies as a living sacrifice, holy and pleasing to God—this is your true and proper worship. Do not conform to the pattern of this world, but be transformed by the renewing of your mind. Then you will be able to test and approve what God's will is— his good, pleasing and perfect will."[55]

These powerful verses became the procedure manual for guiding me through the intricate circumstances of my life. They remind me that by God's mercy, Christ paid the ultimate sacrifice for my sins (past, present, and future), so I could be freely presented as holy before God. However, freedom is never free. Christ paid a painful price to carry my sins on his shoulders at that desolate cross. Because of his selfless act of courage, I stand confident in the presence of God and am transformed.

According to Romans 12, in view of Christ's sacrifice and mercy, we are called to surrender our will and replace it with his will in order to be rendered pure before our heavenly Father. That's our personal, spiritual act of worship. Daily surrendering our lives and our will (our *living* sacrifice) to God is contrary to the world's view that proclaims we are to live for self. Living sacrificially for Christ keeps our focus on him and transforms us to *his* image, not to the expectations of the world. We are changed from the inside out.

The depth of a relationship is in direct proportion to the time put into the relationship. When I spend more time with God, my relationship and communication with God become more authentic. I learn to lean into the power and authority of God and understand the relevance of him in my life. My emotional and spiritual centers are transformed to be more like him.

As caregivers, we offer our lives as a living sacrifice by giving up our own needs, time, money, jobs, health, and freedoms to help someone else who might not be able to thank us. God sees every struggle and every sacrifice. How we walk through this difficult journey is our spiritual act of worship.

I admit I was fearful of caregiving. I was fearful of the changes, sacrifices, and the day Mom would no longer remember who I am. I was fearful it would put a strain on my marriage, my family, and my job. Being fearful is not a sign of weakness—it is merely the beginning of courage and bravery. Caregivers are courageous soldiers who overcome fears and challenges to serve others.

When my dad was living with Alzheimer's, my mom was fearful too. Mom often struggled with the emotional pain she felt when he no longer knew her, didn't remember their anniversary, and couldn't converse anymore. Nonetheless, she was a courageous soldier for Dad. Every day, she drove twenty miles to the nursing home, her car rims scarred from scuffing the curbs on the winding Ozark roads. She wept silently and alone as her journey into depression began again. Recent studies report that spouses of loved ones with Alzheimer's have a six-fold greater chance of developing Alzheimer's from the stress.[56] My mom, the soldier, became one of those casualties.

Maybe you're feeling stuck or challenged because this journey hurts. It *does* hurt. I often cried for the things I lost. But I also rejoiced in the gains. My faith grew. My life has been further transformed by the renewing of my mind and soul. I got to spend the last moments of Mom's life helping to care for her, making her laugh, and seeing her smile. God taught me how to count the gains instead of the losses and unleash the chains of fear holding me captive. And God taught me about being pure in heart.

Jesus instructed that we are to be pure in heart, which is both a one-time transfiguration and a daily transformation. Purity of heart is a difficult virtue to hold in today's environment—the distractions of our time, money, and character create unproductive chatter and deception in our minds and souls.

In this context, the heart represents our emotional center consisting of our thoughts, motivations, attitudes, and character. When something is pure, it is free from sin—unblemished and holy. Authentic purity only exists when your heart and your actions are consistent with being virtuous and having genuine faith.

Being pure in heart means our emotional center is holy. The only way that happens is by experiencing a one-time transfiguration through acceptance of a personal relationship with the One who paid the ultimate sacrifice for us to be free. Christ is our atonement for sin and allows us to be unblemished in God's eyes.

Becoming pure in heart is our spiritual act of worshiping God through daily transformation. It is the continuous purging of our faith from impurities and daily residing in God's spiritual presence. It requires consistent self-examination to purge ourselves of anything that grieves God.

Alzheimer's is a highly combustible disease, effortlessly igniting new fires on a daily basis. My parents became easily agitated and explosive, and I was the one called to plow the fire line to arrest the advance of their suffering. I was challenged to exhibit sacrificial faith while dealing with unimaginable aggravation. But in the process, I learned about refinement through the fires of life and what it means to have a faith that is genuine and pleasing to God. He doesn't require my perfection—only Jesus attained that. But he does require me to show up and be available, with my faith compass pointing to him. To him, it's not *what* I do, it's all about *how* I do it. I can do a lot of good things (the *what*), but if my heart or motives are in the wrong place (the *how*), my faith cannot be proven genuine and will be scorned by God.

Traveling the difficult road of Alzheimer's with my parents involved plenty of detours. Many days were *vacuum cleaner* days where it felt like life was being sucked right out of me. It's easy to complain when life hurts, and no one in my trusted circle could blame me for having a bad day. However, if I allowed my bad days to turn into a *bad life*, this would negatively impact my caregiving, as well as my spiritual act of worship. Again, what's truly on display for others to witness is not so much *what* I do, but *how* I do it.

Recent studies demonstrate the ability of people with dementia to remember an emotion long after they have forgotten the event that triggered the emotion. A study co-authored by Edmarie Guzmán-Vélez, a doctoral student in clinical psychology, was conducted by University of Iowa researchers where individuals with and without a diagnosis of Alzheimer's were shown movie clips that prompted responses of either sadness or happiness. The results indicated that not only did the emotions of those with Alzheimer's last longer than their ability to recall what triggered the emotion (some didn't even remember thirty minutes later ever having seen the movie), the emotion of sadness lasted longer than happiness.[57]

The takeaway from the study is this: "[P]atients with [Alzheimer's Disease] can experience prolonged states of emotion that persist well beyond the patients' memory for the events that originally caused the emotion. The preserved emotional life evident in patients with AD has important implications for their management and care, and highlights the need for caretakers to foster positive emotional experiences."[58]

People with Alzheimer's might not remember specific events or conversations, but they will remember the emotions they attached to those events and will exhibit certain behaviors accordingly. Once again, what's remembered is not *what* is done, but *how* it is done.

"Our findings should empower caregivers by showing them that their actions toward patients really do matter," concluded Guzmán-Vélez. "Frequent visits and social interactions, exercise, music, dance, jokes, and serving patients their favorite foods are all simple things that can have a lasting emotional impact on a patient's quality of life and subjective well-being."[59]

Demonstrating purity of heart as a caregiver is not only pleasing to God, but it has a long-lasting impact. A church is only healthy when its members have pure hearts before God. Likewise, a caregiving relationship cannot be healthy without the caregiver having a pure heart before God and to the loved one receiving his or her care. Even when my parents couldn't remember *what* I did, I believe they remembered how they *felt* about what I did.

Who is a pure-in-heart caregiver? He or she is one who understands that there is purpose in every single moment and conversation, pursues God's truth in love, is thankful in all things, chooses to focus on the gains, submits to others out of reverence to God, is submissive to the needs of others, and understands that a life eclipsed by selfish desires is a life eclipsed from God's presence.

Macular degeneration or cataracts cause the eyes to become clouded over. Good vision becomes eclipsed. Likewise, our spiritual vision can be easily clouded over by distractions and busyness (whether good or bad), resulting in the loss of our spiritual field of vision and ability to *see* God. As a caregiver, I not only tried to manage my own life, but I also tried to manage the life of someone else. My to-do list reproduced exponentially. But I sought to stay focused on the main thing, which is seeking God and being pure in heart.

I *seek* God by spending time with him. I *see* God when I seek him and don't allow my life to be eclipsed from his presence. It's only by being in his presence that I can truly see God. When I seek God with a genuine fire in my belly, I will be escorted into his presence.

I understand how hard it is to be a caregiver. It was hard to divide my time between caregiving and everything else—my husband, children, friends, job, writing, and my personal needs. I hit my exhaustion quota most days. My energies could only go so far.

But I held on to my coveted relationship with God and always received strength when I absolutely needed it. Much of my prayer time was (and still is) in snippets—while I drove, cooked, ate, or tried to fall asleep. I prayed with my mom every night during our evening phone calls, and I prayed silent prayers when Mom struggled. I still pray while I work my full-time job, when I write, and when I go out for walks around the block. I call out to God with praise and with hardship. He sees my schedule. He's a loving and selfish God who enjoys having me check in with him so that I can grow in my relationship with him. God desires that my spiritual vision is 20/20 so I can clearly see his powerful grace at work in my life.

Caregivers wear a lot of hats—life managers, servants, stewards, God seekers, prayer warriors, first responders, grace regifters, and strength coaches. Caregivers are moms, dads, daughters, sons, siblings, grandchildren, aunts, uncles, nieces, nephews, friends, and strangers. Caregiving is a living sacrifice to God and a spiritual act of worship, transforming the lives of those who receive the compassion and care.

Spiritual Authenticity

Spiritual authenticity is being genuine in how we represent our faith, regardless of circumstances. Again, it's not necessarily *what* we do, it's *how* we do it.

Writing the first draft of this chapter took many weeks. Finding the right words and anecdotes became a formidable task, and I got frustrated. A difficult situation caught me off guard and literally brought me to my knees in prayer. Through the anguish, I recognized that God allowed me to labor in my writing because he needed my full attention so I could learn the valuable lessons waiting for me through the fire. Months after finishing this chapter and walking hand in hand with God through the fire, the focus on spiritual authenticity resulted in an unexpected, but much desired, reconciliation with my sister.

The perplexing situation required me to face fears and emotions that had coexisted in me much of my life and that could infringe on the safe zone of my emotional center. I knew that however I responded to the situation, I could either be emotionally wounded again, emotionally healed, or left unaffected and neutral. I was mostly afraid of having the scars broken open again.

It became apparent to me that writing about spiritual authenticity required being willing to live out the virtues of the Beatitudes in all situations of my life. I could write the book (the *what*), but if I'm not emanating the virtues in all circumstances (the *how*), including the fires, my faith is not spiritually authentic. The bigger question was, "How could God use me if I wasn't authentic?" I desperately prayed for answers and told God I was willing to receive them.

Armed in prayer, my husband and I left for church. During our thirty-minute drive to church, I reflected on the Korean War Memorial plaque and the statement that the beginning of courage is fear, and that bravery is how we step over our fear. Through my morning at church, God steered my attention and gave me the wisdom I needed to face the fears of my difficult situation.

**In order to be authentic, live out the virtues and
trust God to assist with stepping over the fear.**

The sermon's focus was all about praying fearlessly and boldly. I was aware of my pronounced, uncomfortable feeling of conviction about facing my fears directly. I was reminded that prayer allows me to put on the spiritual armor to face any circumstance. Without prayer, my efforts are merely efforts, and I lose in areas where I'm not praying enough. Additionally, my passions are revealed in what I pray for. If my passion is for authenticity, I must pray for authenticity. If my passion is to step over fear, I must pray and trust God to give me the courage to do it.

**Pray for courage and bravery to deal with the fear
of doing the right thing, regardless of outcome.**

The day of lessons continued in Sunday school class. The lesson was called "Stand Courageously" (gulp!) and was focused on King Nebuchadnezzar's threat to put Shadrach, Meschach, and Abednego into the fire if they didn't bow down only to the king, which they flatly refused to do. They prayed for bravery to do the right thing, which was to be loyal to God. The king threw them into the fire, which was so hot that the soldiers who put the three men into it were killed from the intensity of the flames.

The king looked into the fire and saw four men, instead of three. God himself was in the fire with the three men of faith. All three prayed for courage and bravery, and they trusted that God would be with them in every fire.

Stand courageously. Then, God can stand with me in the fire.

I wrote copious notes during the Sunday School lesson, including:

> "Even if God does not save me from the fiery furnace, I will not conform and will not deny God. God can bring me through the fire unharmed, unsinged, and unscorched. It's obedience he asks of me. Walk the talk. The flames will be there, but God will protect me. Courage begins with fear. Bravery is the willingness to conquer it and do the right thing. Am I going to trust in the fear, or trust in my God? Put your faith to the test. Let God's light shine.

> "If I show a weakness (a crack in the wall) because of fear, the enemy will surge through and undermine my faith.

> "Our faith and confidence must be in God alone—not only in the furnace, but out of it as well. God doesn't merely protect us from the fires, he joins us in them. Then we can have peace, regardless of the form of the answer."

Trust and choose bravery. Go beyond the fear. God will either deliver from the fire, or will deliver in it. Now that is the ultimate spiritual authenticity.

Suffice it to say, I knew that the decision to take a chance would result in either of two things—God would deliver me *from* the fire (no more wounds) or deliver me *in* the fire (allow me to recognize that my fears no longer held me hostage, regardless of whether I was wounded again or not).

That afternoon, with a genuine heart (the *how*), I was willing to put fear aside, replace it with trust, and do the right thing. With a pure heart, I offered encouragement (the *what*) to someone who was hurting. While it was important for me to offer the encouragement, the most important part of it was the authenticity—a genuine, pure heart. No one needs to remember or know *what* I did; what God will remember is *how* I did it. I was willing to go through the fire to do the right thing.

While the tender and rewarding times of caregiving are rich blessings, the fires and storms could fill up a book larger than *From Here to Eternity*. As a caregiver, if you have dared to enter the fire, you can have the courage to remember you are never alone.

Alzheimer's hurts at many levels. It robbed the life from the two people I loved my whole life, and I choose to believe in God's promise that I will see them again. But it is still just a disease. It's the *what*. How we care for and love our loved ones matters the most. That's the *how*. That's called goodness.

There is a lot to fear about this horrible disease. But *it* taught me that God resides in the fires with me. I can choose to replace fear with courage, and then replace courage with bravery. When I was armed with courage and bravery, I could fill my mom's emotional center with authentic love, and fear no longer could define Alzheimer's or me.

God showed me a number of ways of demonstrating authentic love and goodness to my mom, even through the fires:

Pray: Prayer turns complainers into proclaimers. It keeps me in my relationship with God and allows me to see God in the fires. Praying for my parents drew me closer to them. It kept me actively in the game, regardless how many strikes or fouls were called against me. Praying with my mom every evening gave me an opportunity to keep Christ the focus of our attention instead of her failing mind.

Feel in Control: Author Marc Lewis stated, "Loss of control is about the worst thing that can befall anyone. From age three to age ninety-three, being in control is synonymous with being okay."[60] Alzheimer's robs a person of the ability to feel okay because it doesn't allow a person to maintain control. I tried my best to find ways to give Mom an opportunity to feel she was in control.

One opportunity was to offer "memory moments." Even when my mom could still communicate, she didn't always use the correct words. In her final year, she had little short-term memory capacity and lost more than five decades of long-term memory. But on those occasions when she could remember a daily or lifetime event, we declared a memory moment. When I called her before she went to bed, she was usually tired and her memory was worn thin. But if she remembered something she did during the day, I proclaimed, "Memory moment." She always responded with great joy. In those memory moments, she felt temporarily back in control of her life, even if it was as small as remembering having gone down to play bingo or having a visit from the church ladies, or as large as remembering the story my husband told her about he and his Dad sitting on the porch during thunderstorms. She was grateful to be reminded she still had a little memory and control in her life.

Keep a "No Mocking" Zone: I tried to make sure I didn't mock her attempts to communicate. When I was on a business trip to San Jose, California, I called Mom to tell her I could see the mountains from my hotel window. She asked if the mountains were wide or skinny. I stopped to think about what she was asking. I didn't know if she was asking if the mountains were "big or small" or "tall or short." All she could say was wide or skinny. This is an example of the tangled maze of a mind with Alzheimer's. I simply responded they were stretched out long and not very high. She couldn't get her words out right, but I could help her know I still understood. It reminded me to always seek out her intentions with a pure heart and answer her questions without judgment, which helped her feel more in control.

Feel Needed: No matter how extensive the disease progressed, Mom needed to feel needed. On that same business trip, I had a horrendous headache from traveling and visiting an office with fresh carpet and wallpaper (and formaldehyde). I was terribly exhausted. But I still made my evening call to Mom, and I told her how much I needed my mama. When she asked why, I told her about the exhaustion and the headache. Without pause, she said she would pray for me. She was totally my mom and felt needed and in control.

Avoid Agitation Saturation: We tried to avoid opportunities that could lead my mom to lose control. Until the final weeks of her life, we always brought Mom to church on Sundays. On one particular Sunday, things got quite intense when we brought her back. She was tired from sitting in church and Sunday school. We checked her mail (she got frustrated getting her mailbox open), unlocked her door (she got frustrated trying to unlock her door), read her mail, took down the bird feeder outside to refill it, cleaned up her kitchen, read the note on her table regarding a flu shot and explained to her it was okay to have one, and read through her monthly calendar of events at the assisted-living facility. It was a whole-lot-of-busy before we needed to bring her to the dining hall for lunch, and she reached her saturation point of agitation. I noticed her pupils were small, and she was timidly silent. I knew she felt out of control. I saw the *look*, gently took her hand, held her close, and used the mirroring technique. I spoke to her in a low, slow voice. The more we embraced, the more her eyes grew dilated. Slowing everything down and helping her put things back in control gave her success for the rest of the day.

Another tool to relieve agitation is to create stimulation of the hands. Using motor skills redirects attention away from a source of frustration. We bought my mom a small bag of soft tennis balls and announced she had a new job. We told her the tennis balls simply needed to be squeezed. She smiled as she squeezed them, and we could see the tension being released from her face. Any skill that required her to work the muscles in her hands helped to release the agitation in her mind, including popping bubble wrap.

During moments of agitation, my only recourse was to allow God to breathe goodness into me and help me be a living, breathing grace regifter.

Silliness and Positive Attention are Good Medicine: I loved doing silly, crazy things. If it didn't make my mom laugh, it allowed me to laugh. I threatened to start the shower, grab an umbrella, and sing "Singing in the Rain." We danced and sang to "You Light Up My Life" when it played on the radio. We held hands and looked at old photos. We took her for rides in the car. We frequently told her she was okay and talked softly and slowly to give her a chance to understand us. We tried to find things she *could* do rather than what she *couldn't*.

Step by Step: We learned to explain things in single and methodical steps. The disease destroyed her ability to think in the abstract, and her reasoning skills rapidly deteriorated. She became the child, and we became the adults. For example, when my husband called Mom in the morning, he helped her determine what day it was. We learned we could no longer say, "Mom, your calendar is on your kitchen table. Look at the last date you circled. Take your pen and circle the next day on the calendar. That's today. After you've circled it, come back to the phone and tell me what day it is." Eventually, we simply asked her to grab the calendar and come back to the phone. Then we guided her through each step until the proper day was determined.

Reassurance: During one nightly phone call, Mom was distraught and said she felt awful. She was concerned because she believed there were children in the common area outside her doorway. I asked her specific questions: "Have they harmed you?" "Have they bothered you?" "What are they doing that makes you anxious?" She was anxious merely because they were there. Or she imagined them to be there. I told her they were probably related to someone else at the care facility, she would want her own young family to be welcomed there, they weren't doing anything wrong, and perhaps she didn't need to worry. She agreed, and then she thanked me for reassuring her.

Golden Rule: In all things, we wanted to treat her the way we wanted to be treated. We reminded her she was valuable. And we learned to cherish every moment because there was never any guarantee of how many more moments we were going have. Despite the chaos, I would still give nearly everything to have one more day with my mom, yet I would never want to have her suffer that way ever again. Praise God for the gracious gift of eternity!

My caregiving prayer for you is this: I didn't want to consider caregiving a sacrifice because it seemed too harsh a word for doing what I simply believed was the right thing to do. But the storms swirled, and at times it was agonizing and hard. Sometimes I didn't know how I'd get through it. When I recognized that God's calling for me to be a caregiver for my mom was a living sacrifice, holy and pleasing to God, then I understood that it was all for God, to the benefit of my mom. Making the sacrifice about God instead of about me allowed my faith to be spiritually authentic and allowed my time with my mom to be a rich blessing. I pray that you will look upon this time as a gift to God, a sacrifice that will be a rich blessing filled with memories that will sustain you after your caregiving is done.

~~~~~~~~~~~~~~~~~~~~~~~~~~~~~~

Prayer: Lord, I seek shelter in you because you promise to protect me. You lead and guide me with grace and mercy. Be gracious, Lord. I am worn out from anger and sadness. But I will trust in your plan for me, Lord. The course of my life is in your hands. Thank you for giving me the courage to be fearless. How great is your goodness. In Jesus' name. Amen.[61]

Chapter 8

Rusty Chains

Blessed are the peacemakers, for they
will be called children of God.

Matthew 5:9

But the fruit of the Spirit is . . . faithfulness . . .

Galatians 5:22

If I were asked to describe caregiving in one word, peaceful would not be the adjective I would choose. Granted, there were tremendous times of peace-filled, tender moments along the way, but caregiving for someone with dementia would be better described as chaos—emotional, physical, mental, and spiritual anarchy. Not all chaos is bad. It is just chaos!

No two days were ever the same. The unexpected became the expected, illogical conversations began to sound normal, and schedules were created in pencil. It became impossible to even attempt a description of my day to someone who asked. But for many caregivers and loved ones, the chaos manifests into depression and thoughts of suicide.

In 2013, a study conducted of 120 family members caring for dementia patients revealed that twenty-six percent of those caregivers contemplated suicide, and that thirty percent of those who considered suicide said they were likely to attempt it in the future.[62] Additional studies concluded that those diagnosed with a cognitive disorder, such as Alzheimer's or Huntington's, have an even higher risk of suicide and physician-assisted suicide, particularly when they are first diagnosed.[63] In seventy-three percent of those cases, firearms were the most common method.

Dr. Jack Kevorkian's first physician-assisted suicide took place on June 4, 1990, when he assisted with the intravenous delivery of a lethal solution in the back of a Volkswagen van to a fifty-four-year old English teacher named Janet Adkins. She was from Portland, Oregon, and she was diagnosed with early-onset Alzheimer's. By her choice and by her hand, Janet pushed the start button of the controversial machine that infused the deadly poison into her bloodstream. Seven years later, Oregon was the first state to enact a Death With Dignity Act that made it legal for physicians to prescribe lethal medications for patients with terminal illnesses. There are more states currently looking at approving similar legislation.

I have family, friends, and coworkers who have lost someone to suicide. I personally know a number of people who have contemplated, attempted, or committed suicide, including a friend who used a firearm after being diagnosed with early-onset Alzheimer's. Additionally, I personally understand being drawn to the doorstep of suicide. I was there, and by God's grace alone I didn't enter into the temptation.

I ranked eleventh in my class of nearly eight hundred students when I graduated from high school. I was editor-in-chief of our school newspaper, debate and band trophies collected dust in my bedroom, and my peers in band chose me for a coveted leadership award. My desired vocation went from teacher to lawyer, and I ultimately landed at a college two hundred miles away from home with a plan to major in business.

For the first time in my eighteen years, I struggled with homework. A few of my high school friends were at the same college, but I still felt isolated. Promiscuity and alcohol became my seductions, and living in a dormitory made it easy to succumb to those temptations. I always wanted to save myself until marriage and live to a higher standard. But loneliness and guilt continued to increase in direct proportion to the increased internal struggles resulting from my lifestyle choices.

In the early spring of my freshman year, I started hanging out with the California-based football players down the hall. They respected my decision to refrain from smoking marijuana, but their dorm room was frequently filled with the familiar fragrance. I'm sure I was minimally affected by it. I enjoyed being with them because I felt like I was accepted without scorn or judgment. My secret world of alcohol and promiscuity that cradled me in despair could remain hidden—until the night my sleep was startled by urgent pounding on my door.

I lunged out of bed, opened the door, and wondered why one of the football players stood outside my doorway at two o'clock in the morning. He said he needed to talk to me and wanted to come in. I always felt safe with him and reluctantly allowed him into the solace of my room to determine what was wrong.

He began kissing me in a way that felt very uncomfortable, and I didn't feel safe anymore. I pleaded with him to stop, and I repeatedly said, "No!" But he had only begun his disparagement of my dignity. He pushed me onto my cold mattress. He stole the serenity and comfort of what was once my bed—the only peaceful respite that endured the heavy darkness of my loneliness. Then he leeched what little remained of my innocence—this three-hundred-pound football player raped me. I desperately wanted to scream for help. But I was overcome with shame, convinced no one would ever believe I said, "No!" I kept trying to push him off me, but his daunting weight was unrelenting.

When the violation was completed, he left without saying a word. I silently shut the door as my tears of shame stained the floor. I slowly wrapped myself in my robe, gathered my toiletries, cautiously opened the door to make sure he was gone, and shuffled down through the deserted hallway to the showers to try to wash off the memory of him. I soon discovered I could wash away his scent, but there was no way to wash him out of my soul.

In the morning, the football players apparently went back to California. I never had to see *him* again, even though the memory of him still holds the scar.

I was emotionally tormented by the chaos, fear, and humiliation. A few nights after the insidious violation, I sat alone at my desk. Only the light from my tiny lamp broke the darkness in my mind. (In making a comparison now, I wish I could have broken Mom's darkness in *her* mind.) I felt as though I had let absolutely everyone down—including God. I labeled my life as *failure.*

I started to make a list. On one side of the paper I listed those who were close to me, like my family and friends. It was a short list. Next to each name, I wrote how long I thought it would take until each one would forget me (it's ironic now that my mom appeared on that "forget me" list). Years later, I realized the people closest to me were given the least amount of time until they would totally forget me, obviously because of the inordinate amount of guilt and shame taking up residence in my head.

The next day, I walked over and sat by the big lake adjoining the college property. I leaned against the strong oak tree next to the battered picnic table, and I gazed across the water to the endless horizon. How ironic that such a joyful place for many others became a place of turbulence for me. I pondered what it would feel like to start walking out into the water until I could no longer feel the bottom. I didn't know how to swim. I believed I deserved a painful end to my shameful life. I stared across the water for over an hour, crying out to God because I wrongly believed I disappointed him the most.

Before it got dark, I returned to my room, grabbed my sleeping bag, and left to spend the night on a small public dock to decide my fate. At the dock, an acquaintance walked past and asked if she could join me. I guess she thought it sounded like a great idea to sleep under the stars. Even now, I don't remember anything we talked about that night, or if we talked at all.

Thirty years later, I returned to that campus to face the wounds, starting with the dormitory. I looked up at my dorm window, desperately wanting to weep. But my silent spirit was empty as I remembered the details. I wondered how many other young women were violated there too.

Next, I sojourned to the lake and leaned against my familiar oak tree for the last time. I reflected on the caustic resolve that held me captive decades earlier—the resolve to walk into the water and never cause any more shame to those I loved.

My last stop took me back to the dock. The water appeared much calmer than thirty years earlier—or maybe it was I who had found tranquility by making peace with my past.

I no longer remember the acquaintance's name, but I like to believe God sent her to interrupt my plans that night on the dock. God knew he had a purpose and plan for my life, and he wasn't finished with me yet. He wanted the chance to bring me back to a place of peace and to prove to me that, in Christ, I am not merely the sum of my brokenness.

I understand how badly life can hurt, especially as a caregiver. But Jesus is the ultimate healer. God reaches out to return those in chaos to a place of peace through the Beatitudes' admonition to be a peacemaker.

We don't live in a world defined by peace. Terrorists are in abundance, forty-seven million people worldwide battle Alzheimer's, over a hundred Americans take their own life every twenty-four hours,[64] and divorce separates over fifty percent of marriages. That's obviously only the tip of a large, chaotic iceberg. Yet God tells us not to worry. Philippians 4:7 says, "It's wonderful what happens when Christ displaces worry at the center of your life."[65]

As a card-carrying member of Worriers Anonymous, an admonition to live my life as a peacemaker, rather than one consumed by worry and chaos, seemed quite foreign to me. Yet God calls me to be a peacemaker; in return, he promises to call me his child. My Abba Father wants to replace chaos with Christ, my *soul* peacemaker, so I can regift his grace to those around me who need it.

As a struggling peacemaker, I searched to understand the difference between peace *with* and peace *in* my life. In order to be at true peace, both kinds of peace must coexist. Caregiving for someone I loved so dearly mandated that I discover within myself a place of peace. How could I help my mom find peace if it was lost in my own soul?

Peace "With"

Having peace *with* means being at peace with my mere existence as well as with the internal struggles related to my emotional and spiritual psyche. In order for me to acquire peace *with* caregiving, I first needed to possess peace *with* God, peace *with* myself, peace *with* relationships, and peace *with* the disease called dementia.

Peace *with* God

Peace *with* God starts with a personal relationship with Christ, then stepping aside and allowing him to be in control of the details of our lives. That can be difficult for anyone still impacted by deep, internal wounds from the past. For example, those who were abused or abandoned by an earthly father may falsely assume that God will abuse and abandon them too, rather than display his unconditional love for them. Or those who have been labeled a failure by themselves or others might be mistakenly convinced that they are also a failure in God's eyes.

For years I felt I was a failure. I assumed God didn't need me and certainly must be disappointed in me. Looking at life through a living room window was lonely. The rape was a painful reality of the culmination of my bad choices. My life was far from perfect, and since God is perfect, how on earth could he ever want *me*? Or need *me*? God only wants perfect people, right?

Wrong.

He knew me before I was born. He knew I would sin and fall short. He knew I could never attain perfection on my own. That's why he sent Jesus to take on the punishment I deserved. God takes imperfect sinners and gives them freedom from the rusty chains holding them hostage to their past.

So I asked God to forgive me. He never promised to make my life perfect, but he did promise to accept me *as* perfect because of Jesus.

God wants us to communicate with him always, through prayers of petitions and praises. The more we pray, the more we are drawn into his presence. Regardless of whether life is perceived as good or not good, he is there. He never moves away from us, but we can move away from God.

I've seen large, anchored buoys on several of the Great Lakes. They are secured to the floor of the lake and cannot move. But they can appear to move, depending on where I am in relationship to the buoys and how big the waves are. The bigger the waves, the more the buoys appear to move. In reality, they bob up and down, but they don't move from their physical positions. If I'm distant from the buoys, they look like they are moving. But if I'm close to the buoys, I can see they aren't—I am the one who is moving.

There are primarily two types of buoys—those that are anchored or those that are allowed to drift. God is like an anchored buoy. He never drifts away, regardless of the size of the waves in our lives. The more time I spend with him, the closer I stay with him and can see that he is constant and immovable. God promises that everything comes together for good. He is the ultimate peacemaker and wants us to have peace *with* him. That doesn't mean everything *is* good, but he will use the circumstances of life to draw me closer to him so I will learn how to rely on him more.

God doesn't cause dementia, but he can choose to allow it. I don't have an answer as to why both my parents and a cousin were allowed to walk through the chaos of Alzheimer's, nor why he allows it to impact millions of other families, nor why he may have allowed it in your life. But I do know that the closer I stayed to Jesus, the tighter he held onto my hand as we walked through it together—just like when I held my children's hands when we crossed a busy street. I know God uses painful experiences to draw us deeper into an increased reliance on him. He promises to give us strength when we feel at our weakest.

Making peace *with* God is letting him off the hook for the painful things and faithfully believing he didn't cause them. Making peace *with* God means trusting him even when it's hard to see him through the hurt. Making peace *with* God means coming to him with a humble spirit so he can draw himself near.[66]

Peace *with* Me

In deference to God's promises, I believe he sees all of us as his beautiful creations, flawed by sin, and righteous before him through Jesus. Yet it's normal to find ourselves doing battle with that one thing that has the power to sting us. When it stings, it takes us to our knees, which is where we literally ought to go when we are stung.

What is your battle? Mine is *failure.* That label has been tattooed on me by others and myself. I have allowed it to break me many times. However, no one has the right to put that label on me, including me. I am not a failure before God, nor to my parents, husband, children, and beloved friends. In Christ, I have a firm resolve to keep peace *with* myself and no longer put myself through the paces of doing battle with inappropriate labels or past failures or present disappointments.

I assisted in creating a beautiful handiwork out of the remnant pieces of my mom's broken road through Alzheimer's because I chose to be part of her life's passage. My only failure would have been to ignore God's calling to not let her suffer in isolation. I am far from perfect in the world's eyes, but I am at peace *with* myself. Failure? Not me! Jesus' dictionary doesn't contain the word *failure*. I choose to see my reflection the way God sees me, and I'm at peace *with* that.

Peace *with* a Loved One

Peace offers freedom from distressing thoughts or emotions and grants affinity in relationships. Peace *with* relationships was and remains the toughest one for me to step over.

When I was eight years old, I overheard a discussion between my parents that negatively impacted my life for nearly forty years. My dad told my mom that if I was so sick with allergies (perceived as my failure), I should be put in a hospital so he could have his cigarette-laden, guitar-pickin' parties (perceived as abandonment by a loved one). I felt the pain of both rejection and failure, and that event became a source of abandonment that held me hostage for much of my life. I had perceived that my failure deserved abandonment.

In 2003, I was introduced to Dr. Tracy Kemble and *The Right Living* program. One of the topics in the program is "Healing from Abandonment and Rejection."[67] For those like me who have struggled with rejection or abandonment, those issues have a trigger point or root cause. I learned that if I didn't deal with the root cause and properly pluck it out of my life, I would carry the pain of abandonment with me throughout my life. Jesus can't restore what I don't give him.

Dr. Tracy used the example of a dandelion. I could pluck out the weed and be convinced it was gone forever. But if the root remained, the dandelion would sprout again. In order to heal from an abandonment issue, I must destroy and release both the weed (the feeling that I deserved abandonment) and the root cause (my perceived failure) in order to allow restoration in Christ to replace them. I experienced great healing when I discovered and dealt with the root cause. This healing allowed me to let my parents, and me, off the hook for the comment I overheard decades earlier.

Like me, my parents carried their own wounds and, in Dr. Tracy's words, they could not give to me what they did not have.

My dad undoubtedly felt abandonment and failure when he was ten years old. He had walked home from school and found his house completely empty—no parents, furniture, or possessions. His parents somehow forgot to tell him they were moving that day.

My mom undoubtedly felt abandonment and failure when she was seven years old. After she tried to tell her mother that she was sexually molested by a friend of her mother's, instead of being supportive, her mom instructed her to never talk about it again.

Both of my parents struggled with abandonment issues, and this side of heaven I will never know if either of them was released from the root cause. I am grateful that I was brought to an understanding that my parents could not give what they did not have, because we all live our lives with flawed memories and experiences. I made peace *with* my parents, and they probably never even knew anything was wrong.

There are always hard times between parents and children. When I came to understand the gut-wrenching disappointments in my parents' lives, I was able to comprehend and intrinsically accept that they loved me enough to overlook mine. They nurtured, taught, and loved me. That allowed me to nurture, teach, and love them through anything. We had peace *with* each other. And we enjoyed getting into playful mischief together.

Peace *with* Alzheimer's Disease

Because I have peace *with* God and *with* myself, and had peace *with* my mom and dad, I have no choice but to be at peace *with* the disease. *It* is a disease, and I accept that I hate *it*. I hate that five million Americans have *it*. I hate that I might get *it*. And I hate that *it* stole my parents.

Conversely, Alzheimer's allowed me to become a better woman, daughter, wife, mother, sister, and friend. It also allowed me to become a more authentic child of God as I daily learned how to relinquish more of myself to his will and recognize his blessings for my life. And it allows me to have greater empathy for you and the struggles you may be facing.

Peace "In"

Because I have a personal relationship with Christ, I have assurance I can find peace *in* my external struggles or situations. God can choose to mercifully grant me peace *from* the storms, but I can always secure his peace *in* the storms. When Shadrach, Meschach, and Abednego were thrown into the fire by King Nebuchadnezzar[68], God gave them peace *in* the storm by coming inside the fire with them to protect them from the heat, rather than granting them peace *from* the storm by not allowing the king to throw them into the fire in the first place.

My mom experienced tremendous storms. Some days when her memory was better, she got a reprieve and could stand in the serene eye of the storm. It still swirled around her, but she could live in the moment and be at peace *in* the storm. She could remember where she lived, who her children were, and where to go for fitness class. However, when she cognitively strayed outside the placid eye of the storm, the wind and the waves consumed her. She sundowned, wandered, experienced panic attacks, cried, and thought her children were still coming home from school, and her blood pressure soared to critical heights. She could never stand on the shore and watch the storm go out to sea. But I was grateful for those times when she could return to peace *in* the eye of the storm. Mom never attained peace *from* Alzheimer's prior to reaching her eternal home, but she experienced peace *in* Alzheimer's with help from God, the nursing staff, and her family.

When Mom was consumed by the wind and waves, I reminded her with my words and actions that Jesus said, "No, I will not abandon you or leave you as orphans in the storm—I will come to you."[69] As a caregiver, I relied on that promise and regifted it to my mom. I couldn't heal her memory or her sadness. She felt lonely and abandoned without my dad. But my love never ever abandoned her as an orphan in the storm. I always came to her, in person or by phone. I became the mother, and she became the child. And I promised to never leave her.

On a church marquee, I saw the phrase, "When it's Hardest to Pray, Pray the Hardest." Sadly, my first thought brought me back to difficult times when I could hardly sputter out any words in prayer. At those times, I simply trusted that God knew my heart, even when the words wouldn't come out.

The apostle Paul wrote in his letter to the Philippians that, despite his trials, "I will continue to rejoice, for I know that through your prayers and God's provision of the spirit of Jesus Christ what has happened to me will turn out for my deliverance. I eagerly expect . . . that I will . . . have sufficient courage."[70] During a low point for Paul, he chose to rejoice and have courage because he knew that the prayers of others would carry him through and set him free. Paul was able to experience peace *in* the storms.

What encouragement! Through prayer, our heavenly Father promises we can rejoice in all things and be delivered, courageous, and set free, regardless of whether we receive peace *in* or peace *from* our situations. God answers prayer yesterday, today, and tomorrow, even when we don't know how to pray or when our words only sputter. Prayer is such a vital spiritual discipline that the next chapter is devoted to God's gift of prayer.

Through prayer and God's love, I obtained deliverance and peace *in* all my circumstances of caregiving. It was terror for my mom and dad, and it was terror for me. It was painful to watch those who had cared for me be unable to even care for themselves.

But God is true to his promises, and I was given the strength to have peace *in* caregiving.

Being a Peacemaker

Once I could make peace *with* God, my loved ones, the disease, and myself, and I was able to make peace *in* the turbulence of caregiving, I could throw off my rusty chains and be equipped to be a peacemaker in addition to a caregiver. Scripture says we are blessed to be a peacemaker—a blessing to myself as well as to my loved ones.

One of Patsy Clairmont's best-selling books is *God Uses Cracked Pots*. Through humor, she describes how God shines through our daily struggles and imperfections, and how we can thrive through them and allow God's peace to whittle away at the storms. Being a peacemaker means letting go of chaos, not creating new or additional tensions, and letting the chains of the negative emotions of my past be released from my life.

To survive and thrive, I learned that one of the golden rules of caregiving was to never take a loved one's actions personally. Each caregiver experiences a variety of difficult circumstances: She doesn't mean to cuss in church, be difficult, wear her clothes inside out, or say she's exhausted from babysitting a horse (yep, my mom did all that); or, he doesn't mean to keep you up all night, tell you he hates you, make messes, or incessantly ask the same questions.

I learned how to allow the tender and loving moments to fill up my peace reservoirs so I could draw upon them when the spewing of the disease flew out at me. Mom asked numerous times for me to forgive her for being difficult, not remembering things, or taking up my time. Even when she didn't ask, I forgave and excused her anyway—forgive as Jesus forgives. In reality, I never needed to forgive Mom, but I did have to forgive the disease.

It sometimes felt like I was in the Twilight Zone when I didn't know which dimension of space and time she lived in. Whenever she made calls to me in the early evening, I knew she was most likely sundowning. Even though I called her every night for more than two years, she eventually couldn't remember I would be calling to pray with her, recite the Lord's Prayer together, and comfort her through her difficult emotions. So when the phone would ring prior to my nightly call, I knew she was in a deep struggle. I would take a deep breath and ask God to help me. Ironically, I assigned her with the ringtone of the song "Happy" by Pharrell Williams to remind me to be at peace when she called. It was corny, but it worked for a while. (For two consecutive days shortly after Mom passed away, I heard that song being played while I was shopping, which brought joy, memories, and tears. Four months after Mom's passing, it also brought a feeling of terror and brought me to an emotional collapse when it was played at a Walk Against Alzheimer's.)

On one of her early evening calls, I heard the ringtone, took a deep breath, prayed, and answered, "Hi, Mom!"

She said, "This is your [pause] . . . *really*? I *am* your mother? You *are* my daughter?!"

"Yes, Mom, this is your daughter Cheryl."

"Oh," she exclaimed with a sigh. "That makes me *so* happy. I'm so sorry I haven't been remembering you. I'm so happy to be your mom!"

I had a real conundrum. Did she only *not* remember at that moment that she couldn't remember who I was and now suddenly *could* remember who I was? Or did she really *not* remember me from the prior few months when I called every night, or our weekly trips to church and Sunday school? That was the sundowning Twilight Zone—the conundrum of not knowing if she did or did not know who I was.

What would a peacemaker do? I believe a true peacemaker would say it just didn't matter. I often told my mom to live in the moment (not in the past or in the future), and I needed to do the same. Living in the moment created less chaos in my life and, in the grand scheme of things, in this instance it truly didn't matter. In this particular phone call, my mom exuded great joy because she believed she just found her beloved baby girl. That's more than enough to bring my soul to a place of peace!

Being a peacemaker for others means helping them segregate themselves from the chaos. As a peacemaker, I can disengage from arguing. I can remind them that things are okay and that everything is under control. It became my goal to keep the overwhelming moments to a minimum, which included saying things or offering instructions one at a time, rather than giving a verbal list.

In her final year, my mom still enjoyed doing her own laundry, even though it became increasingly difficult for her to do it on her own. Her failing memory won out over her desired independence. Despite writing it down, she would forget which laundry area she was using, especially if something interrupted her thought process before the laundry was done. She convinced herself that dish soap could replace laundry soap, and nothing I said could change her mind. I relented and resigned myself to the fact that soapy clothes were acceptable.

Mom believed if she could (1) determine which clothes were dirty, (2) put her laundry in the wash, (3) go back to her room, (4) write down where her laundry was, (5) sit in her room until it was done, (6) check her note to see where it was, (7) go back to the laundry room, (8) put her wet clothes in the dryer, (9) return to her room, (10) sit until it was done, (11) check her note to see where it was, and then (12) go back to get the finished laundry, she would be just fine!

Wow, that's a lot of steps, and she was tenacious in her desire to do it herself. What she desired more than clean laundry was independence. However, if anything interrupted her during the process, she forgot about her wet laundry—until hours later. She would then get extremely agitated with worry about the location of her laundry, who was doing it, and when would she get it back.

As dementia progresses, it is tremendously difficulty to maintain abstract thinking skills and perform familiar tasks. Doing something methodically, one step at a time, seems to limit the chaos. I could be a peacemaker for Mom by helping her stay focused on one task at a time and cooperating with her to do things for herself for as long as she could.

Being a peacemaker also means validating fears. Sometimes it was most appropriate, depending on the circumstance, to just tell my mom not to worry because everything was under control. But when we additionally took the time to tell her we understood that it *was* scary to be losing her memory, she felt validated and less afraid. We frequently told her she had a disease that robbed her of the ability to process information correctly, and we would always be there to help her. During those moments, she recognized that she didn't have to feel like she was crazy or stupid.

We enjoyed picking up Mom for Thanksgiving dinner and bringing her back to the home she and my dad built. It was twenty miles from her assisted-living facility. On our final Thanksgiving together, her battle with sundowning began in mid-afternoon. She nervously paced the floors, began wringing her hands, raised her voice, and couldn't remember where she lived. She asked the same questions numerous times: "How will I find my way home?" or "Will you be bringing me home tonight?" or "Do I have pajamas to stay overnight?" or "Where is my purse?" We could see her distress by the deer-in-the-headlights look in her eyes. She was missing more than four decades of memories because she thought home was in Minnesota—eight hundred miles away.

I could have chosen to tell her just not to worry. Instead, I validated her feelings by reassuring her that it was scary to not remember things. I asked her to take my hand, and I led her to my computer room to show her this manuscript and my blog. Our eyes moistened as I showed her the pictures of her and my dad on my blog. She cried as I described this book and how I hoped it would help others through this journey. Mom and I were rewarded with a tender moment between us, and her feelings of being overwhelmed greatly diminished. I reminded her she could always trust me to do right by her. She expressed her gratitude for what my husband

and I were doing to watch over her. Even though she still didn't understand whether she was in Minnesota or in Arkansas, she felt peace in the chaos. We validated her fears, we reminded her not to worry, and we assured her everything was under control.

Finding peace within myself gave me opportunities to share peace with my parents. They needed me to be a peacemaker for them when they could no longer do that for themselves. God holds peacemakers in high regard. He sent Jesus to defeat the enemy of the spirit world here on earth and to be the ultimate peacemaker—fighting the eternal battles we couldn't win on our own.

Children become a reflection of their parents through a combination of genetics and environment. When I stand near any outdoor body of water, from puddle to ocean, I can see my reflection in it as long as there is at least a flicker of light. Even if the reflection isn't an accurate portrayal of my face, there is still a resemblance. Likewise, depending on the situations of my life, I will always resemble one or both of my parents. God's ultimate desire is that my reflection will shine like stars in the sky or beacons of light[71] and that I become a reflection of his image alone. The more time I spend with him, the greater the resemblance.

But life happens. The desired reflection can be tarnished through broken families, disease, depression, bad decisions, domestic abuse, drugs—the list goes on and on. Those are the situations of life in which the weather is stormy, and it becomes difficult to see a clear reflection of all we are and hope to be. When I seek peace *with* and *in* my life, I am able to see the storm clouds break apart. I become a peacemaker—first within myself, and then for others.

When I can reach a place of peace *with* and *in* my life, release the chains and fears of my past, and seek to dwell in the presence of God, I become a child of God because I abide in him with the innocence of a child.[72] As I grow deeper in faith as a child of God living *with* peace and *in* peace, I will reflect more and more the image of God.

Even through the adamantine times of caregiving for someone with Alzheimer's, I still tried to hang on to the peace that passes all understanding and carry with me the promise that I am God's child. But perhaps like you, I succumbed to weeping, mourning, and lamenting. Life really hurts sometimes. In those moments of caregiving, I called out, "Where are you in *this* one, God?"

Young children get scared and call out if they lose the familiar grasp of a parent's gentle hand. They aren't weak; they are struggling. Likewise, when I cry out to God, it's not because I am weak. It is me asking him to show me his pathway, take my hand, and walk me through the struggle. It shows strength in the relationship and draws me closer to him. He will always help me find the calm eye of the storm and moments of peace. His gentle hand will take mine and lead me from fear to blessing.

Faithfulness is a two-way street with God. When I abide in him, he is faithful to abide in me. It is a fruit and gift of the Spirit, and it is to be reflected in my word, loyalty, reliability, and trustworthiness. It was sometimes tough to be faithful when Alzheimer's was such an ostensible adversary.

"Great is Thy Faithfulness" is one of my favorite hymns, and it is rich with God's promises. The lyrics were penned by Thomas Chisholm, and the music was created by William Runyan.[73]

"There is no shadow of turning with Thee"—God never turns his back on me, and nothing can separate me from his love. There is not even a hint of a chance that God will turn away from me in my struggles, or that God would allow anything to interfere with his light or protection in my life. Even the darkness of sin is not allowed to cast a shadow on his love for me.

"Thou changest not, thy compassions, they fail not"—God never changes, and his love never fails.

"Morning by morning new mercies I see"—God never leaves me, and he takes great pleasure in showing his love at work in my life, even when I deserve his punishment. Each day is a new day, and every morning I am assured of seeing God's mercy and grace.

"Pardon for sin and a peace that endureth"—God forgives my sins yesterday, today, and tomorrow, and his peace will never fail nor ever end, enduring through all eternity.

"Strength for today and bright hope for tomorrow, blessings all mine, with ten thousand beside"—God promises to bless me with strength and hope in every tomorrow, and he promises ten thousand more blessings, more than I could ever deserve or imagine.

"Great is thy faithfulness"—God is always loyal to his Word, and I can always trust him to provide what I need in his timing.

What a gift I receive in God's faithfulness to me! He never turns his back on me, he never changes, his love never fails, he never leaves me, he bestows upon me his mercy and grace, he forgives me, he blesses me with never-ending strength and hope, and he is always trustworthy. Even when all else fails, he is constant, consistent, and compassionate. All he asks is that as a child of God, my faithfulness with him will withstand the test of time. He is faithful to take my fear and pitch it from my sight as far as the east is from the west.

The Old Testament chronicles Daniel's story because he was a true hero of faith. He was faithful in worship and in never denying his relationship with God. Daniel kept the focus on his faith.

King Belshazzar of Babylon loved to throw extravagant pagan parties. His final soirée was catered for a thousand of his close, personal nobles. But the feast was disrupted by writings mysteriously appearing on the walls of the palace. The king was in a drunken panic and hysterically called out for someone to interpret what the words meant. He promised fame, wealth, and a pathway to the throne for anyone who could tell him what the scrawls meant. The queen recommended Daniel, who was well-known for his spiritual wisdom.

Daniel quickly denounced the offer of fame, fortune, and royalty. He chastised the king for his arrogance, drunkenness, and contempt for God. To lend insult to injury, Daniel revealed that God himself wrote on the wall that the king's days were numbered, he was despised by God, and his kingdom would be divided up between the Medes and the Persians. The king gave Daniel royal adornments and promoted him to third-in-line in Babylon, despite the ominous predictions.

That night, the armies of King Cyrus and Darius the Mede strategically joined forces to successfully assassinate King Belshazzar in order to restore peace to Babylon. After taking the region without opposition, King Cyrus marched into Babylon and was greeted by the residents as he took his victory lap through the streets.

King Cyrus was beholden to the assistance provided by his Uncle Darius, then sixty-two years old, and commissioned him to be ruler over the kingdom of Babylon. Newly-appointed King Darius was tasked with installing three governors and 120 sub-governors to assist him in ruling the region.

Daniel's spiritual and prophetic wisdom preceded him and, at eighty years old, he was appointed by King Darius to be one of the three governors. He was loved and respected by the king, and he quickly became the king's favorite. Rumors swirled that the king was going to put Daniel in charge of the kingdom.

The other two governors were up to their ears in irate jealousy, and they conspired to concoct a devious plan to dispose of Daniel. They told the king that he had to sign an irrevocable decree lasting thirty days, mandating that anyone asking a favor of God or man other than King Darius would be thrown into the den of lions.

These covetous governors knew that Daniel knelt and prayed three times daily, always with his window open, to thank God for his faithfulness. That night, the conniving duo set up surveillance of Daniel praying and asking favors of God, brought that information to the king, and reminded the king that the law could not be changed.

The king reluctantly signed the order for Daniel's arrest and said to Daniel, "May your God, whom you worship continuously, deliver you."[74] The king sanctioned to have the lion's den sealed so no one could rescue Daniel after he was thrown into the den. The king went back to the palace and restlessly refused dinner, entertainment, and sleep.

While the king was hungry, bored, and tired, Daniel was together with God in the peace of his presence. God didn't remove Daniel *from* the storm, but he did protect Daniel *in* the storm, and his faith was stronger as a result.

Perhaps Daniel's brow was sprinkled with a bead of sweat as the den was sealed and as he thought about those he loved. He undoubtedly collapsed to his knees, praising God for his eternal faithfulness. He knew he would never be separated from his heavenly Father, and he fully understood that this trial of hanging out with big, hairy beasts was momentary. And even the beasts bowed down when the presence of God's heavenly angels was manifested.

In the morning, the king went back to the den and called out for Daniel. The king was elated to hear Daniel's voice saying that an angel came during the night and kept the mouths of the lions shut. The king immediately had Daniel released and issued an edict that the jealous governors and their families were to be thrown into the same den. Hungry from the night before, the lions killed them immediately.

Daniel knew God was greater than anyone or anything that could ever oppose or threaten him. Through his faithfulness to God and God's faithfulness to Daniel, his life was spared. King Darius was witness to God's faithfulness and declared that God alone saved Daniel from the rage of the lions. The king ordered that the eternal God of Daniel was to be worshiped and feared throughout Babylon.[75]

God has proven himself worthy over and over. I know I can always trust that God will never let go of me if I am faithful to him. He knows I make mistakes, and he didn't create me to be perfect. He doesn't expect my perfection. But he does expect my faithfulness for the mercy and grace he gives me, which is far beyond what I could ever desire or deserve—even and especially in the tough times.

Because God is faithful, he will always answer prayers in his timing and on his terms. He will answer with what he knows is best, which can be far different from our expectations. In his great faithfulness, he gives pardon and peace that lasts forever. That's an amazing relationship with an amazing God.

Daniel lived his life in complete faithfulness, and King Darius could not ignore being influenced by the great display of faith by both Daniel and God. Like Daniel, I hope what others remember about me is that they could see my faithfulness. I hope my beacon of light was bright enough for my parents as they battled the most formidable journey of their lives. I hope my faithfulness brought them a feeling of peace that could permeate through even their stolen memory.

Faithfulness takes a strong commitment to loyalty, and it's not always easy.

In all honesty, sometimes my mom was in battle *with* me, but most of the time she was in battle *for* me. I won't recount the argument we had after I gave a formal dinner party for ten friends while she and Dad were out of town and, without her permission, used her antique silver, antique linens, and finest china. That was indeed a battle *with* Mom when she returned, and rightly so!

But most of the time, my mom fought off those who mocked me. She was loyally committed to my future because she unconditionally loved me. I firmly believe that her unconditional love somehow helped her feeble memory remember me until the end. She taught me basic skills like sewing, cooking, and managing finances, encouraged and cheered for my successes, cared for me when I felt sick or alone, and battled to help my life feel normal, despite my obstacles. She even battled my dad when he didn't want me going to France during high school or when she was willing to give me a short-term loan as an adult when I ran short of money.

Perhaps you are one of the many caregivers who didn't experience a commitment of loyalty from the one receiving your care, or never saw him or her model loyalty, yet now find yourself as a caregiver with scars that haven't healed. That's a tough situation for you to step over.

When I faced a loyalty disconnect with my parents, I needed to do the best I could to let *them* off the hook so *I* could return to peace. God let me off the hook for my inadequacies by the sacrifice and resurrection of his Son Jesus. I didn't deserve it because I wasn't always loyal to God, yet he never allows me to stray from his sight. God directed my path so I could find healing with my loved ones.

Many caregivers are caring for those who are too sick to be able to ask for forgiveness or unable to remember what they did that caused pain. Communication might be impossible. If that describes you, by God's grace, there is still hope. A wounded past doesn't have to continue to influence the present or the future. Like my parents, I believe most people probably did the best they could with what they had at the time, and they could not give what they did not have. They were probably wounded too.

Without Jesus, my ability to be loyally committed to others is in direct proportion to the hurts and disappointments I suffered because of them. But with Jesus, the truth is that he nailed my hurts and disappointments on the cross. He died so I could experience his faithfulness and loyalty commitment to me. He desires to see me whole and will help me let go of all the anxieties of life if I ask him. With Jesus, the hurts and disappointments by others don't need to have any bearing on the direction of my life, nor on my faithfulness. The deeper my relationship with God, the more I come to rely on his faithfulness to me.

That's similar in how I cared for my parents. The deeper they traveled through the stages of Alzheimer's, the more they came to rely on me because they were losing so much—from their own independence to their sweet memories of family. Then one day it was over. I have read numerous stories of caregivers who went through tremendously painful struggles caring for loved ones, yet would give everything to just have one more day with them after their loved ones passed away. I understand that now. When my mom was alive,

I got tired of hearing "Happy" when my phone rang because I knew it usually meant Mom was struggling. Now, even with the emotional meltdown of hearing it at the Alzheimer's Walk, I'd give anything to hear that ringtone one more time, knowing it's a call from my mom. But by faith I know where she is, and by faith I am grateful that she is at peace.

Old, rusty chains of the past are heavy, burdensome, and cause anxiety. Until they come off, we are trapped in our life struggles and limited in the peace our lives can enjoy. Life seldom offers a redo. I seek now to live my life without regrets, not placing myself in a position of regretting for the rest of my life what I wished I had done differently.

Faithfulness means remaining loyal to the end. God never fails in his faithfulness to me, and neither was I to accept failure in my faithfulness to my parents. I recognized that being faithful to care for them was much easier if there wasn't dysfunction between us. I released them and myself from the dysfunction by resolving that each day was a new beginning, and I didn't want to be a hostage of my past.

Being able to create good memories while Mom was alive sustains me now that she is gone. Toward the end, she could no longer bathe by herself, her gait stumbled, and her sundowning was the new normal. At church on our final Christmas together, as the congregation sang carols, I took the opportunity to put my arm around her as we sang "The First Noel" together, clearly off-key and at the top of our lungs. Tears began to stream down my face, and I tried to hide them from my mom. But I held her close, allowing the emotions of my love to fill her up. My actions filled up my love tank too, by creating a memory that will stay with me for as long as I have memory.

My caregiving prayer for you is this: We need to be faithful to our loved ones as Christ is faithful to us. That means unconditionally. Our past with our loved ones, whether good or bad, no longer matters. God's faithfulness never fails. Our loved ones have only varying degrees of their past left for them to remember. Be at peace *with* your past and be at peace *in* your tough days ahead. Know how deeply your Father in heaven loves you.

Prayer: O God, have compassion on me. Protect me until this storm passes. I cry out to the God of heaven who can take me to a place of peace. Rescue me from the liars who want me broken. I am surrounded by beasts whose words are sharp like daggers. Lord, your glory is exalted above the highest heavens. You allow my heart to become quiet. I can sing your praises. Your kindness and love stretches further than the universe. Your faithfulness is higher than the moon and stars. Thank you, Father. In Jesus' name. Amen.[76]

Chapter 9

Battle Buddy

Blessed are those who are persecuted because of
righteousness, for theirs is the kingdom of heaven.

Matthew 5:10

But the fruit of the Spirit is . . . gentleness . . .

Galatians 5:23

As caregivers, we are subjected to spiritual persecution, as well
as persecution by others and ourselves. This chapter focuses on
how we are impacted by and protected from spiritual persecution
and oppression.

In my first year of college, we were required to write a term
paper of significant length for an English class. We could choose
any topic, and I chose spiritual oppression. I'm not able to remember
what I wrote. But similar to someone with Alzheimer's, I am able to
remember how I felt.

During the writing of the paper, nightmares woke me every
night and left me gasping and trembling. It's difficult to explain now,
but I felt exactly like the definition of oppression—weighed down
in body and mind and afflicted by an unjust or excessive exercise

of power. I felt darkness, excruciating sadness, and separation from God. It was an emotionally dark and scary place. The oppression ceased after the paper was completed.

Another personal example of oppression was when I was asked to speak at a luncheon at the church where I asked Jesus to be on the throne of my life. I was excited to finally share my faith story at my *home* church. For weeks, I prepared what *I* wanted to say.

Two days before the luncheon, I got sick—total laryngitis. And I truly mean total! I had no voice and practically had to tap out my communications in Morse code! I couldn't fathom delivering a thirty-minute presentation without a voice. My family told me that I'd better advise the church immediately so they could locate another speaker. But I had waited for years to go back to the church that erected the foundation of my spiritual walk and to speak about God's grace in my life. I vowed to trust in how God would work through it, and I never notified the church.

As I approached the door of the church on that Saturday morning, I whispered to the hostess that my voice was weak, but I was glad to be there. I asked for some hot tea and continued to pray through the brunch that God would restore my voice just long enough for the time set aside for my presentation.

I was introduced by the event hostess and began to walk to the podium. I cleared my throat and began to speak—loud and clear! I never used the notes I brought with me. God prepared a message that was far different than the one I had prepared. His words about grace were spoken through my tender voice. When the words I spoke were finished, my voice returned to being raspy and painful. God answered my prayer for a voice—for him. He won the battle against the oppressive enemy who wanted my voice silenced.

As a final example, oppression manifested itself in various ways during the writing of this manuscript. In the course of only two months, I was plagued by a painful and itchy rash over three-quarters of my body. To make matters worse, I experienced vision and pain issues, car problems, work-related chaos, and significant worsening of my mom's battle with Alzheimer's. What carried me through it all was that, in the midst of the spiritual persecution, I sought God's grace.

My personal experiences taught me that the enemy desires to thwart my faith with doubts and lies in order to distract me from seeking God and serving his will in my life. During times of persecution, I know I need to stake my claim in faith under the blood of Jesus Christ. In return, he promises to not allow the battles to consume me.[77]

As mentioned in Chapter 5, when we first moved to Arkansas I began sending up hot-flash prayers when I was awakened many mornings at three o'clock. I anguished over the physical separation from our beloved children, but I recognized that the greatest gift I could give them was my faithful prayers. Our children now ask for my prayers because they know they have become a mainstay of my spiritual walk.

I feel a heightened closeness to God's presence in direct proportion to the expanded time I spend in prayer. When the presence of God permeates me, it is hard for the enemy to penetrate me. The power of prayer protects me from the devastation of spiritual persecution.

Spiritual Persecution

In Chapter 5, righteousness was defined as living a sin-free and guilt-free life in accordance with God's law. The enemy despises when I live a righteous life. He delights in distracting me from living a faith-filled life ensconced in the presence of God by seducing me through debilitating spiritual oppression. In some instances, God and his angels are duking it out in the spiritual realms on my behalf, and I don't even know it. In other instances, God gives me a spiritual suit of armor to protect me in battle.[78]

Providing care for a loved one at home makes it difficult to manage the pressures coming from all directions—often unplanned and always filled with emotions. Energy gets zapped, guilt increases over things that go undone, and anger comes out in unproductive ways. (Anger, in itself, is healthy because it announces that something is wrong either internally or externally. The inappropriate verbal or physical *expression* of a person's anger is what can cause trouble. Abuse is *not* okay.)

Often there was little time for anything other than caregiving (in addition to working, chores, errands, and family). Time with God or worshiping in church became less available, if at all. In the hardest times, I still wondered, *where was God?* Scripture says he never changes and never fails. But aching from the tumult of pressures and energy depletion creates cracks in my faith foundation, allows the enemy to grab intervals of interruption in my life, and compromises my spiritual barricade of protection. That's spiritual oppression and persecution—life feels heavy and weighted down, and my very soul is downcast and drowning.

According to scripture, an unseen spiritual battle is waging war with us. Second Timothy 3:12 says, "Everyone who wants to live a godly life in Christ Jesus will be persecuted." That includes Christians killed for the sake of righteousness, and it includes caregivers. Everyone means *everyone*, including you and me.

The good news is that we don't have to fear, because God's love never fails. Never. Ever. Jesus battled spiritual persecution on the cross and continues to battle it on behalf of you and me. In my weakest moments, the Holy Spirit prays as my intercessor.[79] In my persecution, I fall to my knees and into his presence. My faith is alive and increases when there is nothing else I can do *but* trust.[80] God's will ultimately prevails. Whether he protects me *in* the storms of persecution or *from* the storms of persecution, I am told to be ready, stand firm in my faith, and be equipped in his spiritual armor.

God joins with us in the spiritual battles of our earthly lives and provides all of the proper gear. Have you ever doubted the value of your sacrificial caregiving? That happened to me a lot. In those times, I reminded myself to put on the full armor of God for comfort and encouragement, and to stay in constant communication with him as my battle buddy. I refused to let the enemy steal my joy of regifting God's abundant grace to my parents.

Ephesians 6:14–18 describes the armaments God provides, in spiritual persecution and in caregiving, which include the belt of truth, the breastplate of righteousness, footwear from the gospel of peace, the shield of faith, the helmet of salvation, the sword of the Spirit, and prayer.

Belt of Truth: In battle days, a belt was similar to a girdle and worn to protect vital organs. God snugly wraps me in his belt of truth and wisdom, revealed through the Holy Spirit and God's Word, to protect my vital organ of faith.

Breastplate of Righteousness: In physical battles, a breastplate protects the physical heart. In spiritual battles, Jesus is my spiritual breastplate and protects my spiritual heart. The physical heart cannot function without blood. Likewise, my spiritual heart cannot function without the blood of Jesus, given to me by his sacrificial death and resurrection, through which I am forgiven and cleansed from all unrighteousness.

Footwear from the Gospel of Peace: The wisdom and inspiration in the gospel message of peace through Jesus Christ protects me from stumbling on the seduction of sin. Residing in and meditating on God's Word is the proper footwear to keep my Christian walk from going sideways.

Shield of Faith: In physical battle, a shield is primarily a defensive tool for protection. It is typically attached to the arm or held in the hand. In spiritual battle, my faith in Christ is my shield because it is the cornerstone of my salvation and my eternal inheritance, and it protects me from Satan's attacks that cause me to doubt who I am in Christ. A physical shield can be held in the hand, but the spiritual shield of faith is held in the scars on Jesus' hands.

Helmet of Salvation: Physical helmets protect the brain from physical injury or death. Spiritual helmets protect our minds from spiritual injury or eternal death. During persecution, the enemy attempts to create doubts about our salvation and identity in Christ.

However, by securely fastening on my spiritual helmet, the promise that I belong to Jesus is protected from any deception of the enemy.

Sword of the Spirit: Swords become rusty without use or proper maintenance, and they are used as both offensive and defensive tools. A good example of simultaneous use can be seen in the sport of fencing. The same sword (or foil) is used to defensively protect oneself by engaging it as a shield to stave off the enemy as it advances, and also to offensively disengage the source of the attack through defeat or retreat of the enemy. From a spiritual perspective, if I don't spend time absorbing God's Word, it becomes like a sword sitting on a shelf—rusty, weak, and unreliable. When I consistently study and meditate on God's Word, I'm shielded from Satan's attempts to disrupt my faith and can completely defeat the enemy and bid him farewell to scamper back from where he came. Jesus used scripture to fight off Satan's temptations in the desert. Likewise, the Word of God protects me against strongholds of sin and is a powerful repellant against enemy attacks.

Prayer: All successful battles must employ open and frequent communication with the commander-in-chief. In spiritual battles, I can only experience God's presence through spending time with him in prayer. God is my commander-in-chief. Battle without communication with the commander is called defeat. Battle without prayer is called failure.

My prayer life has dramatically changed. Before moving to Arkansas, the busyness of work, raising children, Bible studies, church projects, errands, charitable causes, and various distractions allowed me to rationalize away the importance of prayer in my own life. My excuse was that I didn't have time.

After his death, working through the emotional loss of my dad and other conflicts in my life made it difficult for me to come to the altar to pray. I hadn't yet recognized that the most significant battle armament God gave me was prayer. Raising my hand to offer myself as a living sacrifice to family, holy and pleasing to God, required time on my knees. I am weak when I fast from prayer. As my mom's condition progressed and I recognized how much the rest of my family needed my prayers, the time spent with my Creator outweighed the distractions.

Caregiving for Mom required difficult choices and sacrifices. A team of doctors and nurses assisted in her care, but eventually either my husband or I needed to be geographically near her all the time because she got more agitated if she knew we were both away. If we were gone for more than a week or two, she sometimes didn't recognize us right away when we returned nor understood how we fitted into her life. Her sundowning periods started by mid-afternoon and sometimes went all day long. She got increasingly suspicious, agitated, and aggressive, and she believed people were making her do things because they didn't like her. Our difficult choices sometimes fell between traveling out of town to enjoy much-needed emotional time with our children and risking that Mom wouldn't recognize us when we returned, or missing out entirely on the pleasures of having time with our children.

For Mom's final Christmas, celebrating for a few weeks in early December with our children up in Minnesota wasn't an option for me. Because we are a blended family, my husband made the trip alone to be with his daughters and grandchildren, and I participated in the opening of gifts via video technology. This sacrifice was seemingly unbearable because it was the first Christmas without my sons. But I knew I needed to stay close to my mom, and I was rewarded with sharing profoundly touching moments with her. However, she routinely struggled to remember if my dad was alive, especially when I brought her back from church, and she pointed to the framed photographs of Dad that adorned her room. She said, "Is that your father? Is that him?"

I spent forty minutes on the phone with her during one of the nights Chuck was away. Literally, every ninety seconds (yes, I counted), she said, "What should I do about your father? Can you tell me if my husband is dead? I don't know where he is."

Mom's experiences sadly reminded me of how my dad went through the same disease in nearly the same way. It brought me to a level of a *new* normal, where a willingness to just let go became a necessity, rather than a luxury. After that forty-minute phone call, I realized through my tears that I was still desperately holding on to her, even though I thought I had released Mom to be with Jesus whenever he called her home.

When Mom lived in the assisted-living facility, she often believed she lived in their motor home and begged not to have to drive it again since she didn't know where Dad was. She didn't know when she'd have to pull out, especially since she had no food or money to stay there or go to the "restaurant" again (which was actually the dining room at the facility). She was scared not knowing when Dad would return from the grocery store with the children after school. This was painful for my ears to hear, in part because she couldn't even remember that she was talking to one of her children!

It quickly became the lesser of two evils to tell Mom that her husband was waiting for her in heaven. When Mom asked, "Why did he leave me," it was easier to say, "Dad didn't leave you. Alzheimer's took him and he's with Jesus." Protecting her from feelings of abandonment seemed to be a better salve for her soul. It got tougher, however, when she said, "I know *that* one's dead, but what about my *other* husband?" We tried telling her she was married only once, but the raw result was the heightening of her agitation. So, we took the shortest route between beginning and end and told her the other one was with Jesus too. We were never certain if she was thinking *young* Dad and *old* Dad, or if she thought *my* husband was her *other* husband. Our strategies changed as her encouragement needs changed. In the long run, we knew she wouldn't remember what we said or did, but she'd definitely remember the emotions she felt.

In these moments, I reminded myself to shroud my fears in the shadow of Jesus and put on the belt of truth (God will never leave me), the breastplate of righteousness (Jesus will protect my heart), the gospel of truth (God will protect me from my selfishness), the shield of faith (Jesus will protect me from doubting who I am in him), the helmet of salvation (Jesus will protect my mind from doubting my eternity and protect me from the enemy's lies), and the sword of the Spirit (to overcome temptation and protect me from strongholds). And in all things, I continued to maintain constant communication with my commander-in-chief. Without it, I knew I'd be open to the counterfeiter who desired to infuse my emotions with lies—"You've sacrificed enough already," or "God doesn't need *you*," or "Do you *really* think you're making a difference in your mother's life?" Spiritual oppression wafted over me in direct proportion to my lack of armor and prayer.

One of the most powerful movies I have ever seen is the *War Room*, which focuses on how to be a true prayer warrior. My hot-flash prayers turned into a deep desire to spend time with the Lord and receive transforming moments of prophetic wisdom, edification, and praise. I learned to treasure the nonjudgmental solitude of my prayer time. I can cry, sing, shout proclamations of gratitude with outspread arms, or listen in silence. It has become absolutely exhilarating for me to pour out my heart to God.

In *War Room*, the main character was coached to construct for herself a personal prayer closet. While her husband was away on a business trip, she decided to use the privacy of her bedroom closet—picking out a spot amongst her clothes, shoes, and laundry. She initially moved a beanbag chair into her prayer closet, but she struggled to find a comfortable position in which to pray without falling asleep (an incredibly funny scene in the movie). She eventually resolved to exclude all luxuries, move everything aside, and use floor space only. Multiple sheets of paper adorned the walls, listing her prayer requests for each member of the family. One by one, she could mark off the prayers as they were being answered.

I'm still searching for the perfect space to construct a physical prayer closet or prayer room, but God and I meet in our spiritual prayer closet on a consistent basis. Prayer is my primary means of communicating with my Abba Father. I limit him if I don't talk with him. My entire life needs to be ensconced in prayer, and I will lose in areas in which I am not praying enough.

When I ask God to show me my true motivations for praying (the "*why*"), he often reminds me to be willing to wait on his timing and accept his answers, even if the answer is "not yet." I recognize I may not always see his answers clearly.

When I ask God to show me my true passions for praying (the "*what*"), he reminds me to take inventory of the focus of my prayers. My passions are revealed in what I pray for. *Am I praying for others? Am I praying for eternal things? Am I praising God in my prayers? Am I praying for grace?*

The enemy can't win persecution battles against me when I surround myself in God's truths through prayer. Lies and doubts are dispelled in prayer. Fears are comforted in prayer. Desires and needs are answered through prayer.

In military campaigns, soldiers have battle buddies who watch out for them physically, mentally, and emotionally. Being a caregiver for both my parents has indeed consisted of physical, mental, emotional, and spiritual battles. God is my spiritual battle buddy. He equips me with spiritual armor and leads me by the power of prayer. Prayers pierce the darkness of evil. Jesus is the light in the world, and evil cannot coexist with the light.[81] Going forward, I know whatever daily struggles I face, I have a divine battle buddy piercing the darkness of persecution. Mine is the kingdom of heaven because I reside there when I pray. Jesus said to follow him, and I will never walk alone in the darkness.

Jesus wanted his disciples to care for "the least of these." For me, that included caregiving for both of my parents. The enemy tried many times to use persecution to try to undermine the Lord's efforts through me. I learned over the years that when God is using me, I can expect the enemy to fight against me. However, God's promise that I will never walk alone in the darkness is etched in my spirit with indelible ink and is stronger than any subversion by the counterfeiter.

God answered my prayer for a voice when I was given the opportunity to speak at my former home church. And he bestowed his favor on me to be the voice for my mother and father through their physical battles. God is my battle buddy, and I was the battle buddy for my parents. I battled in prayer against the forces of spiritual persecution on their behalf as well as my own.

Some days I found myself praying constantly for strength against fear, worry, doubt, and lies. I did prayer walks through Mom's rooms. I prayed that her agitation and confusion wouldn't consume her. I prayed that God's wisdom would fill me, that the virtues of the Beatitudes could be lived out in my life, and that I could regift grace to my mom through the fruit of the Spirit. I prayed when I held Mom's hand in church, when we went for walks, and at her bedside as she struggled in her final days at the hospital. I prayed as I worked, shopped, drove, and did chores. I learned that even through the toughest trials, I could experience heaven on earth in the shortest of prayers or while belting out a lot of missed notes singing "Amazing Grace." God knows my heart—he created it.

When the burdens of being a caregiver were heavy with oppression and persecution, Jesus reminded me that he could ease the emotional and spiritual heaviness by sharing in the burdens with me. He saw every sacrifice I made and every tear that fell. Everything I did mattered to him. He said, "Come to me, all you who are weary and burdened, and I will give you rest. Take my yoke upon you and learn from me, for I am gentle and humble in heart, and you will find rest for your souls."[82] I read this verse many times before I recognized the profound promise and power Jesus offers to those who feel weary and burdened. With my hand prominently raised high and words of praise on my lips, I broke the verse down into four steps required of me to accept relief from the heaviness of caregiving and display an attitude of viable gentleness and humility.

First, Jesus invited me to come to him. He already knew I was burdened, but he still directed me to come to him and ask for his help. As with salvation, Jesus invites me to come, but I must actively accept his invitation to receive it.

Second, he instructed me to proactively take his yoke upon my shoulders. Similar to salvation and the invitation in this verse to *come*, Jesus *offers* his yoke, but I must *take* it. He will never force his will or his yoke on me.

At this point, I logically pondered the question, "What is a yoke?" A yoke is typically a bar or frame resting on the shoulders of two animals so they can work together to carry or pull a load. A yoke doesn't require that the load be equally divided. One who is yoked can carry a greater portion (or all) of the load for the other. In my situation, the wagon represented the burdens of caregiving. Jesus already knew my burdens existed. But when I took his yoke upon my shoulders, I was also asking him to carry a greater portion (or all) of the burden for me, at least for a while. Jesus can't shoulder any burden I don't allow him to take. He didn't promise to end my burdens, but he promised to lighten and transform them into his spiritual purpose.

Third, Jesus told me to learn from him because he is gentle. Again, it required me to take action. He was willing to carry a greater portion of my persecution if I was willing to let him teach me about being gentle and humble in heart. He used my burdens as a teachable moment, so I could learn how to maintain a sense of calm with a servant's attitude in the hardest situations of my life.

Fourth, Jesus promised that if I did those things (come, take his yoke, and learn from him), I would find rest. The burdens still existed, but I was no longer alone in dealing with them. I came to Jesus seeking help with my burdens, yoked myself to him, trusted he would carry me for a while, was willing to learn how to be calm with the heart of a servant, and found respite from the hardships. I took the focus off myself, replaced the focus on Jesus, and trusted him enough to shoulder the burdens with me with gentleness and humility, and without judgment.

Alzheimer's is a malicious disease, ravaging not only the physical victims, but also entire families and others involved in managing its rampages. Even in Alzheimer's, Jesus offered a reprieve from the emotional, spiritual, and mental burdens I carried. I only needed to come, take, learn, and rest.

As Jesus shouldered more of my heaviness, I offered more of my own yoke to my mom and helped her manage the chaos of her disease. Her memories continued to erode a decade or more at a time, and her loss of memory eventually became loss of reality. A little girl replaced the wise adult. Through Christ, and with my help as her battle buddy, her burden was lessened, and I felt it a privilege to be called to share her load with gentleness and the heart of a servant. Some days I could give much. Other days I could give little and was short-fused and agitated. But as I gave more of the load over to Jesus to carry for me, he freed me to carry the load for Mom with a more gentle spirit.

Satan fought to cloud my vision with lies, such as I wasn't doing enough, Jesus didn't really care, Mom didn't know who I was anyway, or that what I did was irrelevant. When those lies hindered my ability to be gentle in carrying the load for my mom, rather than allowing persecution and oppression to erode my compassion for Mom, I went to my prayer room to suit up in the armor of God.

Caregiving taught me that lies lose their power when the light of truth shines through them. God can change any burden into a spiritual purpose because He is willing and available to run any race with me. In all situations, when I'm suited up in the armor of God, spend time in my prayer closet, and ask Jesus to be yoked beside me, lies and fears need not consume me. When I'm yoked with Jesus, a bad day doesn't have the power to steal my gentle spirit or create in me a bad life. And on a good day, his yoke brings me grace and purpose.

Committed to Wisdom, Discernment, and Revelation

Prayer is the pivotal spiritual discipline because it's the primary source of communication with God. Fortunately, it isn't the *quality* of my prayer room that matters to God; it's the *quantity*. Without prayer, the other spiritual disciplines, such as worship, Bible study, or evangelism, would fall flat, and I would be open to spiritual oppression. Prayer is the vehicle God gives me to seek his wisdom (truth), discernment (understanding), and revelation in order to know and recognize his will in my life.[83]

Wisdom is knowledge—the facts and truths that give me the ability to see things the way they really are, or at least as I comprehend them through the filters of my personal life.

Discernment is understanding—the ability to interpret situations or solve problems based on the facts I have been given. Discernment allows me to understand truth by connecting the dots.

Revelation is wisdom or discernment divinely given by God through the Holy Spirit through any means by which he chooses to deliver it.

As a caregiver, I required wisdom and discernment in order to be responsive to Mom's needs, make difficult decisions for her, and better understand the struggles of living and coping with Alzheimer's. On more than one occasion, I threw my hands up in the air or got angry because I simply didn't know what to do next. I was stumped. But since it was my role to serve and protect my mom, I sought help—from my husband, my sister, doctors, lawyers, counselors, and countless other experts, including those who had walked in my shoes. Best of all, I could ask the Divine Expert to enlighten me with his truth, understanding, and revelation to lead the way and reveal things to me I couldn't in my own power even begin to imagine or understand.

Using the oxygen mask example from Chapter 1, I needed to seek God's divine enlightenment in my own life first, before I could pray for Mom to receive his wisdom, discernment, and revelation in whatever capacity she was able to receive and understand them. I had to first strap on my own *lifeline* with God and then assist Mom with hers. Mom and I loved praying together; it was a place we could share where Alzheimer's didn't dictate the boundaries.

Mom struggled with so many things that filled her with anxiety, and she repeatedly asked about them—imaginary people in her room, a perception that everyone hated her, where were her teeth, and so many others. I cried the first time she asked me over the phone, "Where is Cheryl?" But I knew I needed to stay focused on *her* heartache and let my own fade away.

Doctors write medical prescriptions to help ailing bodies. The prescriptions act as intercessors for physical healing and are filled by a pharmacist. As a caregiver, I wrote *spiritual* prescriptions to help my mom's ailing spirit through my intercessory prayers for wisdom, discernment, and revelation. Spiritual prescriptions can only be filled by God and delivered by the Holy Spirit. Through the Holy Spirit, when I pray for wisdom, discernment, and revelation, he unlocks God's special will for my life, walks me through the tender and tough times, leads me to a greater understanding of who God is, helps me care for others, and fosters my faith journey.

It has been said that when we spend considerable time with special people in our lives, we become more like them and can even complete their sentences! The more time I spend connected with God through prayer and the study of his Word, the more he reveals to me. I become more like him. I begin to complete his sentences (with scripture) because I know who he is. My spiritual clarity increases, and I am able to understand his truth, understanding, and prophetic revelation.

When God's still, small voice nearly suffocates me, then I know it's him. When I wake up in the middle of the night in absolute fear and trembling, I know it's likely he's trying to teach me something. When I have vivid dreams or wakeful thoughts, I believe he wants me to understand a truth he needs to teach me. I cannot receive any of this if I'm not immersing myself in a daily relationship with him.

Please don't misunderstand me. I'm a sinner saved by grace who has fallen short more times than there are stars in the sky. But because I *strive* to make it a priority to seek God's face before seeking his hand, invite him into a greater presence in the depths of my life and soul, spend time with him, share him with others by regifting his grace, and keep him on the throne of my life, he knows his divine wisdom, discernment, and revelation no longer fall on deaf ears. I give him more of me, so he can entrust me with more of him.

The deeper I allow my life to be captured by the Holy Spirit directly correlates with how much I experience God's gifts of wisdom, discernment, and revelation. Scripture taught me that the Holy Spirit is the true presence of God residing in me. When I understood that truth, the perspective of my faith radically changed. My dependence on God grew. As a result, I've been experiencing a level of wisdom, discernment, and revelation I never knew was possible except by God's grace. I believe God allows the Holy Spirit to provide us with visions of revelation to convey actions he wants us to take and why he wants us to take them.

Because of an injury to my back decades ago, I find relief in routine therapeutic massage and acupuncture treatments. Months before my mom passed, as I laid on the treatment table during one of my acupuncture appointments, I had a vision of Jesus and me carrying my mom on a white, sandy beach. Jesus was on my right side. Mom was cradled in his arms. My right hand was on his left shoulder, and my left arm was wrapped around my mom as she leaned into me. Jesus did most of the carrying, but we shared the burden. Mom was smiling, and we were at peace. I recognized through that vision that I wasn't expected to carry the load myself anymore. My back began to physically loosen.

Months later, during a difficult massage appointment, and only several months before Mom's passing, my neck and back were excruciatingly tight. My amazing massage therapist, Dawn, was having a tough time getting the muscles to relax. As I laid face down on the treatment table, I began to see the vision I had during the acupuncture appointment. Jesus, Mom, and I were embracing on the same beach, both Jesus and I sharing in carrying my mom. But this time, Jesus began walking ahead of me. I first released my hand from the shoulder of Jesus and kept my hand on the softness of my mom's face. I stopped walking, while Jesus continued carrying her on the white, sandy beach. I released her fully into his arms. Mom turned to me with a gentle, peaceful smile. Suddenly, my back muscles released, and I began to cry softly. At that moment, I asked Dawn if she felt something release in my back. She said there was a significant release of the tension, but I didn't know how to describe what she felt. After the massage was over, I told her what God showed me. We both cried, knowing I had spiritually released my mama into the arms of Jesus and didn't need to carry her on my shoulders anymore.

Jesus understands spiritual oppression because he experienced it. After fasting and praying for forty days and nights in the wilderness, Jesus was tempted three times by Satan. Jesus rebuked the enemy each time with scripture. Satan fled after Jesus told him to leave, and angels came to be with Jesus.[84] What insight we can gain! The enemy typically launches his oppression and temptation when we are at our weakest. But if we have a consistent relationship with the Holy Spirit through prayer and hold a deep knowledge of scripture (the sword of the spirit), we can stand strong and command the enemy to flee. Spiritual oppression is serious business, and prayer and God's Word are the keys to defeating it.

Caregiving often left me weak. I was constantly on standby to render decisions and give opinions about Mom's life on a moment's notice. When my emotional and spiritual reserves ran on empty, Satan's oppression limited my capacity to cope, diminished my ability to be gentle with my mom and others, and weakened any desire to be gentle to myself. When I visited Mom with a depleted spiritual reserve, my spirit ran cold, and I would be short with Mom out of my own exasperation over her questions, her fears, and my sadness over the disease.

In those times of oppression, the fruit of gentleness was in hibernation. It was still in me, but it was dormant. Since people with Alzheimer's will remember emotions long after they can remember events, I didn't want Mom to feel unloved because of my shortness with her. I wanted her to know I was still her gentle, loving daughter. My mom deserved gentleness and kindness in the same generous amounts that she gave me when I was child, no matter what I was spiritually facing.

There is great peace when I walk in cadence with my heavenly Father and he blesses me with his wisdom, discernment, and revelation. I started to chronicle parts of my mom's Alzheimer's journey, and I divided my journal entries into the three components of wisdom, discernment, and revelation. On May 20, 2015, I outlined an entire tender phone discussion with my mom. When I read it recently, I wept uncontrollably because God allowed me to connect with my mom again, and it brought back the beautiful memories of when she had an hour of total clarity and could tell me her desires in the tough decisions we were facing.

In the *wisdom* section, I wrote down just the facts of what happened that day (for example, "Mom asked if her husband was alive," or "Mom thought I was a young child and was waiting for me to come home from school," or "Mom asked me that when she gets mean, if I will forgive her").

In the *discernment* section, I wrote down my thoughts or feelings, the progression of the disease from my perspective, or what I learned about what happened that day (for example, "When Mom's pupils grow small, it means she's agitated, and I need to gently calm her down," or "Mom complains of being lonesome because she can't remember seeing anybody").

In the *revelation* section, I wrote down the ah-ha moments—the actual moments of divine revelation or what I believed God was teaching me for edification or direction for others (for example, "He revealed details to me about my mom's passing before it happened," or "God already showed me what to do—all I have to do is have the confidence to execute").

I included in my journal both prayers I prayed and answers I received, which God used to encourage me and to help me care for my mom. But there was little time left most days, and I didn't put added pressure on myself to write every day. Sometimes I merely jotted down notes of significance that helped me to see patterns of my mom's behaviors, her progression with the disease, and right decisions about her care. It helped me to see how much God was in the *middle* of this journey with me, not merely watching from a distance. And it's heart-warming to have her with me again when I read through the journaling I *was* able to do.

When the geographical distance first separated me from my children, I learned that the greatest gift I could give them is prayer. When mental distance separated me from my mom, the greatest gift I could give her was prayer. And when spiritual distance tries to separate me from God, the greatest gift I can give myself is prayer.

My caregiving prayer for you is this: We have the privilege of building a relationship with a living God through communicating with him and learning what he teaches us through scripture. Prayer, reading scripture, and journaling build that relationship. He wants us to spend time with him as often as we can, but he understands that time is at a premium for caregivers with many responsibilities. My prayer is that you come to him, take his yoke, and learn from him, because it is in that yoke where you will find rest and protection against oppression. Stand firm. Your spiritual battle buddy stands at the ready.

Prayer: O God, I am grateful that your perfect love casts out fear. Thank you for your promise to shield me and be my refuge. You are my rock, my strength, my freedom. You equip me for battle and uphold me through persecution. Do not let me grow faint and stumble. Praise be to the rock of my salvation, the one who loves me with unfailing love and who fights against the enemies of darkness. In Jesus' name. Amen.[85]

Chapter 10

Two Plus Two Equals Forgiveness

Blessed are you when people insult you, persecute you and
falsely say all kinds of evil against you because of me. Rejoice
and be glad, because great is your reward in heaven.

Matthew 5:11–12

But the fruit of the Spirit is . . . self-control . . .

Galatians 5:23

Before my husband and I made the decision to move to Arkansas,
one of the attorneys I worked with was leaving the firm and was
active in the Alzheimer's Association. I knocked on her office door
as she piled up her boxes and asked if she had a family member with
Alzheimer's. She gently put down the box that was cradled in her
arms, and we began to share our stories. She too lost a loved one
with Alzheimer's.

I said I was thinking about moving to Arkansas to assist my
mom. Our conversation hastily turned to a discussion of how
Alzheimer's creates division in a family. I held back my tears as she
told me how disjointed her family became and how it seemed like

a battlefield rather than a coalition as the progression of the disease unfolded.

I was without words—my naiveté was exposed. I was inclined to think it would have been a unifier in a family to have someone "step up to the plate" for the sake of a loved one. I didn't exactly anticipate I'd be nominated for induction into an "Alzheimer's Caregiving Hall of Fame" (if there were such an organization for the heroes of caregiving). But I was shocked to hear that family members, coworkers, employers, and friends could tear down someone who is willing to sacrifice his or her life to care for someone else. Since that tear-filled conversation, I've heard stories, read reports, and experienced the depth of the stress and earthly persecution of caregivers.

The MetLife Foundation funded a study in 2009 in which it was estimated that nineteen percent of all American adults contributed to unpaid care of a loved one.[86] That's nearly one in five people! So I looked at some of the costs (related to finances, stress, health, and relationships) of caregiving. Many of these costs are a direct result of the dysfunction and persecution created within families when one member is caregiving for another.

Finances: American employers recorded losses of between $17.1 billion and $33.6 billion annually in lost productivity due to employees who were caregivers.[87] Employed caregivers may lose as much as $659,130 in a lifetime because of reduced salaries and benefits,[88] and sixty-eight percent of caregivers reduced or adjusted their work schedules to accommodate their caregiving responsibilities.[89]

Stress: The Alzheimer's Association lists ten signs of stress that are common for dementia caregivers—denial, anger, social withdrawal, anxiety, depression, exhaustion, sleeplessness, irritability, lack of concentration, and health problems.[90] As I looked closely at these top ten signs of caregiver stress, it seemed more like I was looking at the top ten signs of grieving—absolutely *not* just a coincidence! And it's no wonder caregivers feel stressed—they are! Within two weeks of my mom's passing, I began to sleep better, my thyroid "woke up," and my blood pressure went back down to normal levels.

Stress in caregiving rarely leaves because caregiving can interrupt anything at any time. Stress is created through the deterioration of the loved one, including personality changes, medical issues, emergency room and hospital visits, incontinence, wandering, an ever-changing perception of reality, complaining, depression, unpredictable sleep schedules, "losing" things, anger, breaking things, and teaching and re-teaching mundane tasks, as well as the caregiver's heartache over gradually losing the loved over a long period of time.

Sixwise.com suggests tips for reducing stress and depression related to stress, such as pause and calm down, breathe deeply, exercise, eat healthy, meditate or pray or journal, lie down and rest for a few minutes, stretch, and get enough sleep.[91] However, for many caregivers, most of those tips seem to only make an appearance on their bucket list.

Health: Caregiving is crippling—body, mind, and soul. A majority of caregivers attempt to work a full-time job while providing twenty or more hours of care each week. This results in more illness, disease, and trips to doctors and emergency rooms for *themselves*— assuming the caregiver finds time to address his or her *own* medical needs! In addition to jobs and caregiving, most caregivers have to also manage their own personal households (bills, children, groceries, laundry, cooking, cleaning, and more), leaving little time for exercise, healthy meals, or relaxation. Health declines as isolation increases through the loss of time with spouses, adult children, and friends. My full-time job was forty to fifty hours a week, and caring for mom was easily twenty. I'm still discovering how much my health was impacted from caregiving.

Relationships: Caring.com conducted a survey of the impact of caregiving on marriages.[92] Out of the three hundred caregivers responding to the survey, eighty percent said caregiving put a strain on their marriages. More specifically, the survey discovered that

"25% of divorced baby boomers said caregiving played a major role in their divorce."

My husband and I married in 2009, within weeks after I placed my dad in a nursing home as he entered late-stage Alzheimer's. Our marriage has always been defined by caregiving, either for Dad or for Mom. We are currently discovering our "new normal" and reestablishing the romance that originally brought us together. Fortunately, our four children were already adults when we moved to Arkansas, but we missed a lot of their life experiences.

In addition to the significant toll on caregivers in the way of finances, stress, health, and relationships, there is persecution. The previous chapter focused on spiritual persecution, and this chapter is dedicated to earthly persecution—self-persecution of caregivers, self-persecution of loved ones with Alzheimer's, and targeted persecution by others. Stress and persecution seem to go hand in hand because the enemy can use earthly persecution to serve an evil purpose.

Self-Persecution of Caregivers

Sometimes we can be our own worst enemy. When we are drained emotionally, mentally, spiritually, and physically, it increases the susceptibility to experience *triggers*, which are situations that set off emotions that may or may not even be the *root* of the true emotion. Susceptibility is increased for a caregiver because of the emotional investment with the family member for whom they are caring. In Chapter 7, I discussed the Guzmán-Vélez study that states that emotions are remembered far longer than the original event that triggered the emotions. That study correlates to triggers, and I'd like to share a personal story about one of my triggers.

When I was growing up, Dad frequently yelled at me for being messy and leaving papers all over the house, even when most of the papers were his. I grew up thinking that being messy meant failure. As a caregiver, Sunday mornings were hurried in order to get ready, grab some breakfast, pick up Mom, and arrive at church on time.

Sometimes I liked to take shortcuts, particularly with my hair. So one windy morning I decided not to spend time styling my hair. I let it go *au naturel* and fun.

When we brought Mom back to her room after church, she was having an agitation saturation spell over a number of things. She said, "Why didn't you do anything with your hair? It's messy." Her comment triggered a swift kick of emotion in me. I felt like I let her down—again. Once *messy*, always *messy*. Once a *failure*, always a *failure*. Fortunately I released it right away and, with humor and a hearty laugh, I tousled my hair and told her it was my *fun* hairdo. She meant no harm, she couldn't have even remembered my messy paper days, and she certainly no longer possessed the abstract thinking skills to equate messy papers with fun hair. However, the mere mention of the word *messy* momentarily triggered the root emotion that made me feel like I once again was a failure. My painful emotional reaction wasn't caused by my messy hair; rather, the pain was caused by the emotion attached to feeling like a failure. Releasing it with humor was truly the best medicine, and it instantly dissipated.

The stress of caregiving allows suppressed emotions or unresolved issues to rise to the surface. Loved ones complain, argue, cuss, and then ask, "Who are you again?" If a trigger unleashes an unresolved issue with a loved one, the stress of caregiving makes it even easier to believe in the lies orchestrated by the disease. In my situation, the stress allowed me to equate messy with failure as it related to my hair.

Mom rarely got confused about who I was. But when she did, I needed to choose what I was willing to believe—whether I was going to think she never loved me and that's why she forgot, or if I was going to defeat that wrong thought by rightfully blaming the disease. When she scolded and cussed, I could believe the lie that I had somehow failed, or I could be grateful that I could still be the one to hold her hand and soothe her anxious mind. For a caregiver with an unresolved abandonment issue, being told by the loved one to "get out of here and leave me alone" could be a trigger to reopen the abandonment wound.

When caregivers face unresolved issues, resolving or releasing them is best. One way to do that is to seek logical truth and to pray for God's healing through wisdom and discernment. I've also learned that negative, triggered emotions need to be released as they come up and not stored for later. A sense of humor comes in handy.

Caregivers need to give themselves a lot of grace in order to love themselves like God does. They are doing a job no one else can or is willing to do. Caregiving is hard enough. Self-persecution makes it harder. Shame and guilt need to be purged. *Should* is a word of *shame* and needs to be removed from a caregiver's vocabulary. Being present in a loved one's life is a priceless gift.

My caregiving prayer for you is this: If there were bad experiences with the person for whom you are caring, pray for grace and a forgiving heart. This is a heartbreaking situation. You can survive and thrive, even through this. Do your best to live one moment at a time and release yourself from previous bad experiences and triggers. God knows your inner struggles more completely than you do. Perhaps in his love for you, through the caregiving experience, he hopes to release you from the rusty chains that have held you hostage your whole life. You are offering much sacrifice, and God wants to offer much grace.

Self-Persecution of Loved Ones with Alzheimer's

It is hard for me to grasp what Alzheimer's *feels* like. I know what it *looks* like and what it *sounds* like. And, I know movies attempt to *portray* what it feels like to have it. But unless I have it, I can't know how it feels. I can't grasp how the fear feels, how the fog feels, how it feels to lose all the memories of life, and how it feels to not understand most things that used to be routine.

Persecution is probably the worst for the person fighting the disease. At least as a caregiver, I possessed the mental capacity to sort through facts in order to determine an appropriate response. For my mom, her world became upside down. Her former profession was as a bookkeeper. It was difficult to admit when she lost the ability to work with numbers and that she was becoming increasingly delusional. On one of the nightly calls about six months before she passed, I apparently interrupted her as she was putting her checks in numerical order and balancing her checkbook. That would have been great if she still wrote checks or maintained the ability to balance a checkbook. The disease even took away Mom's perception of reality.

When my frustration level got to the point of wanting to throw things, scream, or run away, I paused to remember the chaos that had become Mom's new reality. Mom was persecuted by a disease that stole decades of her former life. I learned to reflect on Alzheimer's from my mom's perspective, regardless of my own chaos. If I reached my own point of agitation saturation, I tried to diffuse it with the same formula I used on my mom: Pause. Pray. Respond.

Even though I was the caregiver, I was not center stage. My persecution absolutely paled in comparison to what my dad and my mom went through. The disease was center stage, and my parents played the starring roles.

Other Persecution

The MetLife Foundation study of 2009 cited that eighty-six percent of caregivers care for a family member and that nearly half of them felt they didn't have a choice in being the caregiver. There is an abundance of unselfish reasons why no one else is available to care for an ailing loved one—children, distance, job, or health reasons. But there are also plenty of selfish or emotional ones.

Caregivers are life managers who are largely overwhelmed with never having enough time in a day. They pay a huge price—financially, physically and emotionally—to care for someone with Alzheimer's. Stress and persecution are at an all-time high. Yet the same people who don't offer assistance are often the ones at the front of the line slinging words of condemnation, selfishness, and failure. God sees every tear, hears every plea, and offers his strength and empowerment.

Caregiving is a calling God places on a person's life, and callings often coexist with anxiety and fear. When Jesus' mother, Mary, first learned she was going to conceive the son of God, she was terrified and anxious. But she yielded to God's calling, visited her cousin Elizabeth (see Luke 1:46–55), and described her calling to Elizabeth as a privilege to serve God. Mary knew she was abiding in the presence of God and that her experience would also bring many more into his presence. Mary successfully put her initial anxiety and fears aside, despite the fact that I'm sure there was much division and anxiety amongst her family as the news of her unexpected pregnancy became the talk of the town.

Even with all of the persecution, fear, anxiety, stress, and costs, I wouldn't have traded anything for this tender journey with my mom. God's calling allowed me to not only experience the peace of his presence in unimaginable ways, but his calling also allowed me to bring my parents into his presence. I trusted God's promise that he didn't want me to be a slave to fear. As a result of trusting, the journey with Mom resulted in a miraculous, complete restoration of a broken relationship with my sister just four weeks before my mom passed.

Why is there so much division in families over this horrendous disease? God gives us insight through the faith and forgiveness story of Joseph, son of Jacob. Only through humility and forgiveness by all parties in an unforgiving relationship can the full circle of forgiveness be completed and the bond unconditionally restored.

Jacob is believed to have been ninety-one years old when his eleventh son was born. Jacob's favoritism toward handsome Joseph was undeniable. When Joseph was seventeen, God gave him two dreams. He told his brothers that the dreams symbolized that they would one day bow down to him. Not a great decision on Joseph's part, especially while wearing a coat of many colors that his dad made only for him. His brothers and their pride had no intention of ever bowing down to their arrogant kid brother and were jealous that God gave him prophetic wisdom. They were all bitterly jealous of Joseph's strengths and gifts. He became persona non grata because they perceived him to be the favored son of both their earthly father and heavenly Father.

A few weeks later, while the brothers were watching their father's flocks, Joseph went to join them. The brothers were perturbed at seeing him in the distance and spontaneously developed a plot to drop him into a dry well, leave him for dead, and tell Jacob that a ferocious animal killed him. Joseph arrived expecting warm hugs from them. His brothers instead maliciously tore off his coat and threw him into the cistern, despite Joseph's frantic pleas to stop. Filled with remorse, Reuben tried to convince the others not to harm their brother, but the plot prevailed until it was interrupted by a caravan of Ishmaelite merchants.

The jealous brothers relented and agreed not to kill Joseph, but they struck a deal with the merchants and sold him as a slave. The entrepreneurial brothers took his coat, smeared it with goat blood, brought it back to their father, and told Jacob an animal had attacked and killed Joseph. How the web of lies and division continued to grow. What intense grief Jacob painfully endured because of his sons' jealousy!

The merchants sold Joseph to Potiphar, the captain of the guard for the Pharaoh of Egypt. Joseph developed the acumen of a leader, quickly found favor with Potiphar and was placed in charge of everything Potiphar owned. Joseph also found favor with Potiphar's wife; she became quite flirtatious with Joseph. When he scorned her advances, she told Potiphar that Joseph tried to rape her. Joseph was immediately imprisoned.

Joseph again found favor—this time with the jail warden. It was obvious to the warden that the Lord was with Joseph, and he appointed Joseph to be in charge of the other prisoners.

Sometime later, the Pharaoh needed assistance interpreting two dreams, and Joseph was asked to help him. Joseph elucidated the dreams, telling the Pharaoh there would be seven years of great abundance, followed by seven years of famine, and that God revealed this through the Pharaoh's dreams in order to save Egypt. Joseph was released from prison and, at only thirty years old, was appointed second in command under the Pharaoh.

The Pharaoh decreed that multitudes of grains be placed on reserve during the years of abundance. When the hardship of the famine struck, Jacob learned he and his sons could purchase grain from Egypt. He sent his sons (except Benjamin, who was Joseph's only full biological brother) to travel to Egypt to purchase grain from Zaphenath-Paneah, which was Joseph's Egyptian name.

As Joseph prophesied years earlier, the brothers bowed down to Joseph when they arrived, even though they didn't recognize him. But Joseph recognized them. Through an interpreter, he accused them of being spies and jailed them for three days. After the three days were up, Joseph tested them saying that if they were honest men, they would leave one of their brothers in prison as collateral while they brought the food back to their family. Joseph additionally instructed that the brothers must return with their youngest brother, Benjamin.

Reuben reprimanded his brothers, "I told you so. We are being punished because Joseph pleaded with us for his life, but we wouldn't listen." The brothers still didn't recognize Joseph, nor did they realize he could understand every word they were saying.

Joseph turned away with tear-filled eyes as his brother Simeon was bound and jailed. Joseph was no stranger to imprisonment—he was innocently imprisoned by his brothers and by Potiphar. Watching Simeon being unjustly thrown into jail may have triggered Joseph to relive the emotional trauma of what his brothers did to him. He might have wept from overhearing that Reuben tried to save him from his brothers' scheme—perhaps Reuben and the others had an attitude of repentance? Maybe Joseph wept from a heavy heart after he threw his brother Simeon into prison as ransom for Benjamin. His tears might have been in anticipation of seeing Benjamin again. And Joseph undoubtedly battled with wondering whether the brothers would even come back or abandon Simeon like they did to him.

The brothers returned to their father with the food Joseph provided. Reuben told Jacob that Simeon was being held in prison until they returned with Benjamin. Reuben offered his two sons as collateral to Jacob, but Jacob adamantly refused to risk losing Benjamin. Simeon was relegated to a longer prison sentence alone.

When the food ran out several years later, Jacob instructed the brothers to get more. His son Judah reminded Jacob that they couldn't get any more food unless they returned with Benjamin. Jacob agonized over the thought of losing yet another son. But he relented and sent Judah, Benjamin, and the rest of the brothers to buy more grain. Joseph was overcome with emotion upon seeing Benjamin and rushed away to weep in private. Joseph loved Benjamin dearly—it had been nearly two decades since they last saw each other. Joseph surely wept because he knew it wasn't time yet to reveal his identity to his family. Perhaps the tears also fell because his brothers passed his test and kept their promise to return with Benjamin in order to release Simeon.

That evening, Joseph and his brothers enjoyed a royal meal. He resisted the urge to reveal his identity, but he did ask about his beloved father. And he planned one more test for his brothers.

After dinner, while the brothers were preparing to leave, Joseph ordered his staff to fill the brothers' bags with grain and to place his silver cup in Benjamin's bag. After his brothers left, Joseph commanded his staff to chase after the brothers and search in their bags. Upon discovering the silver cup in Benjamin's bag, the staff brought the brothers back to Joseph and were ordered to leave Benjamin with him.

Judah told Joseph of his covenant with his father that he would bring Benjamin back to him and that he gave Jacob the collateral of his own two sons. Judah bargained with Joseph that he was willing to become Joseph's slave if he would please let Benjamin return home. Judah explained it was imperative for the well-being of his father and his own sons that Benjamin return, particularly since Jacob had already lost his son Joseph.

Joseph was struck by the brothers' change of attitude and commanded his attendants to leave, allowing him to be alone with his brothers. He wept loudly as he revealed his identity to his brothers, specifically reminding them that he was the one they had sold into slavery. Perhaps his tears enabled him to release the pain he felt about the actions of his brothers. Now, as his brothers stood before him, he knew the power resided with him to either save, starve, or imprison them. His brothers plotted to kill him, but here they were standing before him with hearts of humility and forgiveness.

Perhaps Joseph wept because he was overwhelmed by God's grace and protection, recognizing that God allowed all of his life's events to take place in order to save his family and a nation. He reminded his brothers what they did. But he also told his brothers to forgive themselves for their actions by saying God led him to Egypt in order to save their lives.

Joseph was now free and reunited with his family. He wept as he embraced his brothers. And he undoubtedly wept because he knew he could soon see his father.

God turned into good the dysfunction and division in Jacob's family. There was certainly plenty of it to go around! Despite the dysfunction, Joseph became a strong leader, his brothers repented, and Joseph could offer them refuge from the deadly famine.

The relationship between my sister and I was fractured for many years, including during the years of caregiving for our parents. I heard many sermons and read a number of Bible studies having to do with the issue of forgiveness. I even taught classes in the area of forgiveness. But as God instructed me to go deeper into this subject through a study of Joseph, particularly because so many caregiving families are divided, I adjusted my thinking about what makes true forgiveness possible and what to do if it is not. My mom always desired that my sister and I patch things up. By God's grace alone, Mom lived barely long enough to see for herself God's total cleansing and restoration of our relationship. And the story of Joseph played a key role.

For many years, *religion* taught me I was required to forgive everyone who hurt me so I wouldn't be the one being held hostage, *regardless of the choice by the other party.* Religion was telling me to forgive the other person, even if they never asked for forgiveness nor displayed true repentance. Try as I might, I would say I forgave so-and-so, the chains were broken, and I no longer held myself captive. But did I really feel free? No! I felt shame because I still didn't feel free, and I still didn't feel like forgiveness really happened. As a Christian frequently does, I thought I forgave myself or forgave the other person, without their knowledge or assent, and then picked it up again and felt ashamed for not being truly forgiving.

Shame and *should* are not biblical tenets of a spirit-filled life! I finally got to the point where I admitted that the mere phrase of "I forgive so-and-so but can't have a relationship with them" made me feel like a failure again. Being told by religion that I was obligated to forgive so-and-so made me feel like a doormat—and a guilt-ridden doormat at that!

My sister battled stage-three colon cancer just months before our reconciliation. I knew my frailties and called out to God with a contrite and transparent request. I told him I couldn't do forgiveness on my own with my sister, and I quite frankly didn't know how to try. I asked him to change my heart if this was in his will. I asked him to instill in me a desire for reconciliation and then show me a pathway for success.

Unbeknownst to me, at the same time, God was also speaking to my sister by planting in her heart a desire to reconcile with me. When God is working on both parties in a conflict with the same thing, there is no denying God. Both my sister and I developed a strong desire to reconcile with each other, even though neither of us knew what God was doing in the other.

God answered my prayer by giving me a desire to release the past. Through my study of Joseph, I discovered that the two components for achieving true reconciliation in a relationship are humility and forgiveness. Both are required by all parties in the broken relationship. One party might carry a bigger burden of humility, and another party might carry a bigger burden of forgiveness, but both components are required. In Joseph's case, the brothers needed to come to Joseph with humility, and Joseph needed to be able to come to the brothers with a forgiving heart. Two parties plus two components equal true forgiveness and reconciliation.

I now recognized why I frequently got stuck in thinking that God required me to simply forgive everyone, especially if they didn't ask for it. To me, it felt like they were all receiving a free hall pass while I was stuck in detention! One-sided forgiveness can be steeped in failure. One moment I can feel that I've forgiven someone and discover moments later that I'm still angry and unforgiving. It can become a revolving door that feels more like shame than forgiveness.

Not everyone in a relationship is always willing to reconcile with both humility and forgiveness. What God showed me is that in order to avoid being stuck in my own life, I needed to learn how to at least *release* someone from what they've done. It requires me to be the only participant. Release alone is not reconciliation, but it removes the chains from obstructing me from being able to move forward. Release sets me free.

Armed with the desire to allow God's will to intercede in the relationship with my sister, I knew I could release the emotions of the past. That one was within God's and my control. I released her and the infractions from my soul so I would no longer be stuck in emotional bondage. If I still felt resentment at times, it didn't mean I didn't release. It merely meant that there was still pain, and God could help me with that. Release empowered me to let go and move on with my life, regardless of the actions of anyone else. It was a guiltless first step, and it allowed me to move forward.

Six weeks before mom passed, my sister came to town to see Mom and with a desire to reconcile with me. God had already helped me release the pain, and I knew that if Lori and I both came to each other with humble spirits seeking forgiveness, I was equipped to offer both release and real forgiveness. Both she and I needed to be humble, and we both needed to be forgiving.

When Lori and her husband drove up to our house, I knew from the moment my sister and I hugged and cried and hugged and cried that all was humbly forgiven between us. We talked about a few details of our relationship over the next few days, but we mostly just agreed that we loved each other and that digging into the past was unnecessary. I was floored by God's perfect orchestration of a delicate plan. But he had two willing participants filled with release, humility, and forgiveness.

Mom actively saw our healed relationship, and we kept telling her we had it right this time. My sister and I hugged and cried on Mom, reassuring her that we loved each other like crazy. I've never seen my mom any happier than she was in knowing that her two daughters, through God's grace, were eternally reconciled. When our mom went to heaven four weeks later, we were able to hold each other up in our sorrow, rejoice in the Lord's timing, and laugh ourselves silly till the wee hours of the morning while looking through family photos.

The bottom line is this: Forgiveness is always the goal for God. He loves me so much that he allows me to ask for one step at a time. For me, the first step was to tell him that I didn't know if I could do it, but I would be open to him giving me the desire for a restored relationship. I admitted to God that I couldn't do it on my own. I gave him a mustard seed from my soul, and with one small seed, he gave our entire family a story of reconciliation, which has branched off to other family members and gave peace to my mom before she passed.

My ah-ha moment concerning release was also demonstrated in God's forgiveness. Jesus' death on the cross released me from my sin and was an offer of forgiveness. Release of my sin opened the door, but it was one-sided. My relationship with God wasn't restored until I humbly asked for forgiveness, desired to turn away from my sin, and placed Christ first in my life. Release opens the door to restoration. Humility and forgiveness are required to seal the deal.

Through the story of Joseph, in addition to uncovering the two components of humility and forgiveness, God outlines two other secondary components—accountability and testing.

Joseph held his brothers accountable when he revealed his identity and reminded them that he was the one they sold into slavery. Joseph reminded his brothers what they did wrong, but he forgave them anyway. Romans 5:8 also includes a caveat of accountability when it says that while we were still sinners, Christ died for us. God reminds us that our sins are still wrong, but he forgives them anyway. Additionally, Joseph tested his brothers to make sure they were genuine and authentic, and God tests us to make sure our faith is proven to be genuine and authentic.

I know I'm one of the lucky ones who was able to experience total restoration of a familial relationship. I'm aware of many caregivers who experience caustic family relationships that impede the ability to caregive, heap on additional stress, and take a heavy toll on the loved one who needs caregiving. My hope is that Joseph's story can be helpful in determining if release, and ultimately reconciliation, is possible in those circumstances. I do know anything is possible so long as it is taken to the prayer closet—when in doubt, pray it out.[93]

What causes earthly persecution in caregiving, including when non-caregivers refuse to become involved? Not everyone understands how painful the journey is for both the loved one and the caregiver. Sometimes God allows these situations for deliverance down the road (in Joseph's case, his earthly persecution was allowed in order to deliver people from famine). There are unlimited reasons for earthly persecution, even of beloved caregivers. Through it all, I try to keep in mind that those who want to live a godly life in Christ Jesus will be persecuted.[94]

Jealousy: The "Father Always Loved You Best" Syndrome

Joseph's brothers were jealous of him because they felt that Jacob loved him best. Like Joseph's experience, jealousy in a family can be caused by various factors, including family dynamics, illness, birth order, intelligence, step families, income, and achievements. There can also be jealousy in friendships ("I don't get to see you anymore") or even work relationships. Most of the time, jealousy is created only in the minds of the beholder, not by the object of the jealousy.

In caregiving, the person receiving care often needs to be the top priority. Whether reality or not, if non-caregivers *feel* they are always second best, they may plot to undermine the caregiver, just as Joseph's brothers wanted to undermine his influence with their father in hopes of elevating their own status. Additionally, if non-caregivers perceive they have failed in their own lives, they may desire to see the caregiver fail too.

Jealousy also can have a component of competition for affection. Non-caregivers may be jealous when a loved one responds more affectionately to the caregiver, rather than to them. This kind of jealousy clouds the fact that it's really all about the loved one. I didn't take care of my mom to win over her affection. I already had that. I cared for her because she needed my help.

Faith and the "Holier Than Thou" Syndrome

Persecution can occur in situations where the caregivers are Christ followers and the non-caregivers are not, and it's not always a result of spiritual persecution. It can be the result of fear or jealousy.

There have been times in my life, including in caregiving, when I've been shunned simply because I profess a living faith in Jesus

Christ. That can be scary to many unbelievers. They don't want their life choices judged or challenged by God, so instead, they become uncomfortable being exposed to the light of faith and offer persecution instead of compassion.[95] Or, a non-caregiver could also be jealous of a caregiver's faith.

Those living without the compassion of Jesus can feel a huge void in their lives. If they don't have compassion, they can't give compassion, which is a top ingredient to possess when caring for someone with dementia.

I don't like being persecuted for my faith, but I recognize that it's part of the journey. Rather than settling in and accepting it, I pray to grow stronger in my faith and that those who are persecuting me can find freedom in Christ and be open to truth.

Pain and Unresolved Conflict

Everyone is shaped by the kaleidoscope of circumstances in their lives—emotionally, mentally, spiritually, physically, and financially. Non-caregivers by choice or by circumstance are no exception and cannot be expected to give what they do not have.

If there are unresolved issues between a non-caregiver and the loved one, particularly for someone with dementia, it becomes increasingly difficult and eventually impossible to seek resolution of the conflict directly with the loved one. The disease becomes an impenetrable wall and can create persecution by the non-caregiver of both the loved one and the caregiver.

If there is unresolved conflict between a caregiver and a non-caregiver, they both owe it to their loved one to try to work things out, or at least to develop a strategy that allows the best for their loved one. Practically speaking, caregiving is a full-time job and doesn't allow a whole lot of time for working through a lifetime of conflict with someone else. Joseph is an awesome example. While the ultimate result in his situation was complete forgiveness, he was willing to be satisfied only with release. He didn't seek out his brothers, and he didn't know they would come to him seeking food, except for the dreams God had given him. He stayed focused on the fact that living out God's calling in his life was more important than the issues with his brothers.

I can't heal others; they need to work through their own wounds and avoid causing persecution, preferably with God's help. In those situations, I can pray that God's unending grace will prevail and bring about a healing of the wounds.

Fear: "O Brother, Where Art Thou?"

Fear creates persecution.

When Jesus and his disciples arrived in the territory of the Gerasene, an unclothed, demon-possessed man left his residential cave in order to meet Jesus. Jesus commanded the demon to leave the man, but the demon said, "What do you want with me? I beg you in the name of God never to torment me."

The demon told Jesus his name was Legion because there were many demons. The demons begged Jesus to let them enter the pigs feeding on the hillside. Jesus did so, the legion of demons entered the pigs, and the pigs rushed down the bank into the lake and drowned. The demon-possessed man was instantly healed. Those tending the pigs saw the miracle and ran into town to tell everyone what they saw. The townspeople rushed to see what happened, only to find the formerly possessed man sitting at the feet of Jesus, fully clothed and with a sound mind. The townspeople were terrified instead of grateful, and they asked Jesus to leave.[96]

Sometimes when the disease of Alzheimer's enters a family, some will desire to put the loved one with the disease in isolation—not because it's contagious (which it's not), but because they prefer to believe it doesn't exist. It creates fear in many.

Non-caregivers might fear that their loved ones won't remember who they are. They may fear there's not much they can do, it won't be appreciated, and it will take up too much of their time or money. They may fear the depth of the grief over the long goodbye.

Non-caregivers may fear they will end up with the disease, or they don't want to see how dreadful dementia can look. They fear they will be hurt by the loss because it can't be cured and death is the end result.

Non-caregivers may also fear the stigma of dementia—not wanting to be embarrassed in front of others by behaviors of the one with the disease, or humiliated by any social discrimination resulting from having the disease.

Non-caregivers may fear the responsibility of protecting their loved one from the consequences of wandering, sundowning, or getting lost. At times, it is truly like caring for a young child.

What casts out fear? God's abundant love.[97]

As a caregiver, God called me to accomplish a task of compassion and to be intentional in caring for my mom, not flee from fear. Some will flee because it's uncomfortable. In the above story, the townspeople fled because they were uncomfortable with their fears. Others may flee, but never Jesus. He came to cast out fear.

Those with dementia have much to fear—why things are missing and who is stealing from them, abandonment because the people they knew decades ago have disappeared from their lives, getting lost because they can't remember where they're going or where they came from, and having to live years with the horrible disease.

Showing God's unconditional love to my mom undoubtedly meant more than I could ever imagine. If love casts out fear, which I believe it does, it was a privilege to be the one to regift God's unconditional love to my mom. I am convinced Mom could remember the emotion of feeling my love without remembering specific events because I steadfastly remained present in her life.

Mom watched me as I moved about a room, held on tightly to my hand as we walked, followed me wherever I went, and her eyes lit up when she saw me—even to her final days. I got to be the world

171

to her. I am convinced that she could hang on to love, which gave her brief respites from the fear.

Selfishness: "Drama Queen"

Selfishness and guilt can fuel persecution.

Because humans are flawed, they offer excuses to relieve them from a promise or an obligation. A prime example is when I'm running late, which is one of my chronic vices. Very few excuses are valid because it's my own fault for not leaving early enough. But out of guilt, I call anyway, apologize, and let them know I'm on my way.

I was recently running late for an appointment. I called and said, "I know you've heard this one a *hundred* times (drama), but I'm honestly running a little late because I'm stuck behind a funeral procession (guilt)." To make matters worse, this was the first funeral procession I was in since my mom passed away. Not only did I feel guilty for being late, I was emotional as I remembered watching the cars pull over in honor of my mom's procession, which is a law in Arkansas. Guilt and drama go hand-in-hand with excuses, even when the excuses are valid. But it still didn't change the fact that I was late because I didn't leave early enough, and I felt guilty.

Many caregivers have family members living within a two-hour radius from their loved ones. This can be tender luxury when they offer to help. But often times the non-caregiving family members will fabricate dramatic excuses, such as they can't take off work or afford the travel expense, their children's schedules conflict, they promise to come later, they have a medical appointment, they need to walk the dog or do the laundry, or they're leaving for their big anniversary trip to Africa. All of these can be considered a luxury by caregivers who can't get away for a vacation, go to their child's school play, see a doctor, sleep, or walk through the house because the piles of laundry are too high.

Sometimes excuses are honest ones, but other times they are selfishly born out of a fear of losing control or appearing weak.

Non-caregivers might fear losing control of their time, emotions, finances, or freedom. They may worry their lives will be disrupted. They may dread visiting their loved ones and not being remembered. And they certainly don't want to appear weak by allowing someone else to tell them what to do.

A lack of participation in care can be valid. My sister couldn't participate while she battled stage-three colon cancer. But leaving a loved one's life entirely is not okay. Sharing the burden allows for sharing the blessing.

When I experienced earthly persecution, I reflected on how Jesus suffered far more than I ever could. He was put down, insulted, thrown out, lied about, ignored, and killed. His mere existence made others feel uncomfortable. Scripture tells us that when God's children are persecuted for doing the right thing, all of heaven applauds.

I believe that the Beatitudes relating to spiritual and earthly persecution also apply to caregiving. Caregivers are the hands and feet of Jesus. When I suffered persecution for caregiving, I was persecuted for God's calling on my life. Knowing I was called, I aimed to keep my focus on my greater reward in heaven. I clung to God's presence, and he gave me the power to persevere during difficult times. And all of heaven applauded.

I had a front-row seat to dementia's dramatic performances and watched my parents cast in the starring roles. Act One started out slowly, with memory lapses, wrong words, and losing things. Many times laughter could mask the denial that my parents had Alzheimer's. But as Act Two began and the disease progressed, neither laughter nor denial worked to alleviate the reality. The normal of having more good days than bad rapidly changed to the new normal of more bad days than good.

Watching dementia's progression is like watching a boulder starting to roll down a hill. It rolls slowly when it's first dislodged. But it picks up progressively more speed and destroys more things in its path, and it cannot be stopped until it reaches the bottom. Memory lapses become memory losses, wrong words become gibberish, and losing things becomes losing the memory of those things. Dementia is a rapidly increasing destruction of the mind.

I suffered persecution by others, and I suffered the persecution of watching the disease consume first my dad and then my mom. God saw every moment of my caregiving and the emotional pain I went through. Through every joy and every tear, I experienced his abundant grace by drawing closer to him through the virtues of the Beatitudes and learning how to embody a faith-filled life through the fruit of the Spirit. And I got to live my life regifting his priceless grace to my parents during the toughest years of their lives.

The last fruit of the Spirit is self-control, which means self-restraint, willpower, and level-headedness. Not exactly the top three descriptions of my character! But they are certainly valid requirements for caregiving and persevering through persecution.

Joseph stayed intensely connected with God despite persecution by his brothers, Potiphar's wife, and others who were jealous of his leadership skills. He held fast to his relationship with God, exhibited the consummate level of self-restraint and willpower when his brothers asked for help, and faithfully completed God's plan for saving Egypt.

Joseph was chosen by God, and I have come to believe that every caregiver, including you and me, has been chosen within God's plan. He knows me from the inside out and prepared me before I was even born. God knew all of the bumps and bruises I would take on through living out his plan. I am convinced that when I am faithful to my calling, I cannot fail. He is faithful to give me the strength to walk through anything, as long as I keep my eyes and my heart focused on him. And he offers me a yoke with him to share in my burdens.

After Jesus fed five thousand people with only five loaves of bread and two fish, the disciples took the boat and went to the other side of the lake while He dispersed the crowd, went up the mountain, and prayed into the night. Before dawn, a strong wind came up, and the disciples screamed for help. Jesus left the mountain and walked on the water to reach their boat, which was out a considerable distance. They were terrified again because they thought they were seeing a ghost. Jesus told them not to be afraid.

Peter asked Jesus, "If that's really you, call me to join you on the water." Jesus told him to join him. Peter jumped out of the boat and began walking to Jesus. When Peter realized he was actually walking on water, he got distracted by fear, began to sink, and cried out for Jesus to save him.

Jesus said, "You of little faith!" He grabbed Peter's hand, and they returned to the boat as the winds subsided.[98]

In this faith scenario, Peter asked Jesus for a calling and a word. Jesus called out one word to Peter, "Come." Peter heard the calling, he received the word, and he obeyed the word. When he set out of the boat and was focused on Jesus, Peter walked on his word and stayed on top of the water. When Peter got distracted by his surroundings and took his eyes off Jesus, he started walking on the water, rather than on the word, and he started to sink.

What does this teach me? It teaches me that when I affirmatively respond to God's calling on my life, more than ever I need to keep my eyes on him, not on any surrounding distractions or storms. Peter went on to become the recognized leader of the disciples. Even though he stumbled on the water when he was distracted from the word, he knew his calling and lived his life exuding it. Peter also learned that Jesus is always—always—right there to grab us if we start to fall or sink.

Caregiving taught me to never take my eyes off Jesus, no matter how tough the storm. I must reside in my prayer closet and in the Word of God. Keeping my eyes on Jesus allows him to take me by the hand to safety no matter what I face.

I lost my first child in miscarriage. If you have also lost a child through miscarriage, you and I know exactly what this loss feels like. When I called my girlfriend in tears, no words needed to be said. She walked that road several times, and she just knew. She cried with me. Those who had not lost a child in miscarriage were sympathetic, but they couldn't comprehend what the big hole in my heart really felt like.

Dementia is the same way. I was an eyewitness to what dementia looks like and sounds like, experienced the myriad feelings of loss and grief, and learned exactly what it feels like. My heart aches for a caregiver who cares for a loved one with dementia—we're both members of a club we didn't ask to join. Those who never personally knew someone with dementia cannot possibly know how deep my emotions ran. They can't experience the hole in my heart as I watched my parents fade away. Some who don't know someone with dementia may choose to persecute caregivers, sometimes without even realizing they're doing it. In those times, I fixed my eyes on Jesus, just like Peter. Jesus never lets go. He is no stranger to heartache, rejection, and persecution, and he knew exactly what my loss felt like.

Caregiving was God's plan for me, just like God had a plan for Joseph, his family, and all of Egypt. When I found myself alone and isolated, I remembered God's words that said he placed me there "for such a time as this." He placed me at this time and in this place for his purpose because it was the right thing for my mom.

Mom and I were always close. We were best friends and shared many mischievous adventures together. Joseph told his brothers not to be angry over what they did to him because it was ultimately God's plan and the best for their family and for Egypt. Because of my special relationship with my mom, God's choice for me to be her primary caregiver was truly the best for Mom. So I learned not to be angry under persecution, just like Joseph. I passed the test, but I fell far short of acing the exam. The ultimate calling on my life was to provide support and compassion to my mom. It was a tough journey, but the memories it created were priceless.

And in all things, I tried to be grateful. Mom deserved my self-control and doing the right thing, even when it was difficult. This was Mom's journey, and God placed me there to help her handle the road.

Self-control is essential to surviving persecution, and it's also required in caregiving. Dementia is a progressively exhausting disease that wears down caregivers in various aspects of their lives. So I focused on several questions: How am I going to live my life? How do I want to finish the race? What kind of a legacy do I want to leave behind?

My husband and I stood firm in our commitment to Mom. We wanted to serve the Lord.[99] We wanted to finish strong. Our children and grandchildren were watching not only to see *if* we finished the race, but they were also watching to see *how* we ran it. Only God knows if our children were watching how we cared for Mom in preparation for how they may have to care for us in the future. Because both of my parents have passed from Alzheimer's, my chances of developing it are increased. I pray with all my heart that my children won't need to care for me. But if they do, I would like to believe that God can show them the way through it because of how they witnessed God in us.

My caregiving prayer for you is this: God has sent you to rescue the quality of life for your loved one. Your sacrifices and your tears have not gone unnoticed. He's counting on you to finish what he ordained you to do even before you were born. Keep your eyes on the one who sent you.

Now, that's the race I want to finish. The prize of heaven greeted Mom, and it will one day greet me.

And you.

Chapter 11

I Called Her Mama

Praise be to the God and Father of our Lord Jesus Christ! In his great mercy he has given us new birth into a living hope through the resurrection of Jesus Christ from the dead, and into an inheritance that can never perish, spoil or fade. This inheritance is kept in heaven for you, who through faith are shielded by God's power until the coming of the salvation that is ready to be revealed in the last time. In all this you greatly rejoice, though now for a little while you may have had to suffer grief in all kinds of trials. These have come so that the proven genuineness of your faith—of greater worth than gold, which perishes even though refined by fire—may result in praise, glory and honor when Jesus Christ is revealed.

1 Peter 1: 3–7

"This is the nursing station. We need to talk to you about your mom."

The phone call I dreaded interrupted the monotonous clicking of my keyboard and announced that my mother's final journey had begun. She fought the good fight, and it was time for her to go to her eternal home. Alzheimer's was finally being defeated by grace.

Again. The angel God sent to earth to be my mom, my best friend, my biggest fan, my protector, and my defender was being set free to go home.

"Her chest x-ray shows some kind of a mass, and her blood oxygen is at near fatal levels. She's been struggling and is asking about you. We told her you're on your way. She immediately relaxed, but we'll be taking her to the emergency room." I took solace in knowing that the sound of my name brought comfort to my mama, and that she still remembered me.

As I nervously gathered up my things so I could leave for the hospital, I got an urgent phone call from our attorney's office. "The hospital just called to ask if we could send over your mom's living will. Is it okay if we do that?" Through my tears and angst to leave the house for the thirty-minute drive, I told her to please send it over to them. I took a deep breath, raced out the door, and jumped into the Jeep for the treacherously emotional drive to the hospital. While Mom was raced to the emergency room, I raced like Jeff Gordon to meander the twenty-five miles to the hospital through the Ozark hills.

My husband was in Wisconsin, preparing for Fourth of July weekend with our children. I stayed back to care for Mom. I called him from the car, needing to hear his compassionate, reassuring voice. "Please call over to church and get someone to meet me at the emergency room," I told him. "I can't do this alone." Such prophetic words! We exchanged our love, he prayed, and I vowed to drive safely.

My steering wheel became wet from the flow of my tears. I bargained one last time with God. "Lord, you've been faithful in preparing me for the last six months to feel like I could be with someone when they pass. You know how much that terrified me. But you prepared me, and the fear disappeared. Jesus, please don't take Mom until I get there. You promised me I could be with her. Please, God, let me be with her!"

My heart was lighter, and I knew God would honor my plea and allow me to hold my mama's hand one last time. My mind now had a chance to reflect on how God had been preparing Mom and me for this moment and the frantic drive to the hospital that seemed to last for a thousand miles.

The Dream

I thought about our December 2014 pre-Christmas visit to Minnesota. Early one morning, I woke Chuck to tell him, "I had the dream." I often wondered if I would have a dream about my mom similar to the one I had about my dad as he gazed into heaven wearing his blue jeans and white V-neck T-shirt. In this December dream, Mom was slowly walking down a corridor with stoic elegance. She was young and slender, and her long, black wavy hair gently swayed as she approached the door. I looked past my mom and saw a bright light eclipsed by a figure in the doorway. He was waiting at the gates of heaven for my mom. They never took their eyes off each other as mom slowly reached towards my father.

Church

In her final two months, Mom frequently fell asleep for brief periods while we sat in the pew during church services. Then she would become alert and lean forward, reaching out for something that only she could see. One Sunday as she tried to grasp onto something in front of her, I quietly asked her what she saw. She said she saw a light. I asked, "What kind of a light, Mom?" She said, "Bright light. Like a flashlight." When the service was over and we began to stand, Mom said, "Wait! We have to wait for your father. He was just here. Didn't you see him?" Who was I to question?

June 10

Our family made the decision to admit Mom to the psychiatric floor at the local hospital for medication reevaluation. She was disrupting the male residents at the nursing home, convinced they were all my father and yelling at them for not listening to her. Her anxiety levels were frighteningly high, and she was nearing the final stage of Alzheimer's. The medications that worked in the past were no longer keeping her at a functional level.

We walked Mom into the hospital and up to the sixth floor lock-up unit. She was fully ambulatory, able to communicate, and at times could understand that a medication change might help her. But it was hard for me to accept that I had to leave her in a locked unit with restricted hours of visitation. I was used to having complete access to my mom, and now there were rules that said I couldn't have that any more. After spending a little time with her, we were told it was time to leave. My gait was slow to the elevator, and I couldn't even bear to look at my husband. I felt so guilty.

June 12

The new medicine was beginning to make her less aggressive, but excessively groggy. Mama and I cuddled side-by-side on the couch and held hands as she gently fell asleep on my shoulder. I emotionally embraced that special moment, believing it would be my last birthday with her, and I memorialized it forever. I kissed her gently and allowed her peaceful sleep to consume us both. On this day when I was born, she held me. On my final birthday with her, I was holding her.

June 15

I was called into a conference with the psychiatrist, the social worker, and one of the charge nurses to discuss Mom's care and prognosis. My sister participated by phone, and I was quite unsettled when the doctor asked if there was anything they needed to know about my mama to assist them in helping her. I told them I thought she had lost at least six decades of memory, bringing her back to her teenage years or younger.

I stammered as I knew what I needed to reveal next—to the doctor and to my sister, who never knew what Mom shared with me years earlier.

"Mom was seven years old when she was sexually molested by a man her mother knew. When she told her mother about it, she was told to never, ever bring it up again. Mom was abused, and then she was shamed. I'm concerned the disease has brought her very close to the decade of when that happened, and it may be contributing to her agitation. I think she remembers the emotion, but maybe she can't remember what exactly happened to her."

With tears and deep sobbing, I apologized by phone to my sister for never telling her. The millstone of my mama's darkest secret crushed my spirit. I never *ever* intended to tell anyone.

After the conference, I was allowed to visit with Mom briefly, even though it was outside the restrictive psychiatric visiting hours. Most of her communication was now gibberish. The millstone grew larger.

An alarm monitor became Mom's best friend. It alerted the staff anytime she tried to squirm her way out of the chair that held her hostage. The medications created unsteadiness in her gait, and she had already fallen twice. The millstone now became the size of the Grand Canyon.

June 18

Visiting with my mom became increasingly difficult. I could hardly understand anything she said. But I still searched for silly moments to get her to laugh.

During my ninety-minute visit, I watched in amazement as my mom and another patient participated together in a hallucination. The other patient gently held an imaginary firework in his hand, and he steadfastly looked at it with amazement. He offered it to Mom, who took it from him and began to study it with her fingers and her eyes. As I watched, I was speechless. I had never seen two people share in a hallucination together! After they were done, I assisted her as she tried to figure out how to drink juice with a straw. Then she hollered out, "Where do I have to go to get a beer around here?" She was planning to go out drinking with her girlfriends and hoped not to run into some guy named Eugene who was pushing her to try smoking. It is said that exercising the brain can diminish the risk of developing Alzheimer's. My brain was truly exercised in trying to decipher Mom's thoughts through her gibberish.

I left in a daze and found myself thinking in "nonsense-ese." I left the hospital to go the local health-food store just five minutes away. As I pondered which zucchini to buy, a voice in my head carried on quite a nonsensical conversation over which zucchini was better and happier. All I could do was shake my head and laugh, and recognize that a five-minute drive just wasn't long enough to reset my brain. A young clerk named Andrew asked how I was doing. I began sobbing, and he hugged me. Laughter began as I explained the intriguing talk I had with myself over zucchinis. Sometimes there's solace in the stupid things.

June 25

Mom's birthday allowed moments of fun to cut through the darkness. I brought her brownies and cards, along with hugs, kisses, and smiles. I phoned Chuck and, by speaker phone in front of the other patients, we sang the worst version of "Happy Birthday" imaginable. I laughed as Mom sang along, not even certain she knew it was *her* birthday. All the patients and their visitors applauded and generously lavished her with birthday greetings. She smiled broadly and giggled like a schoolgirl.

Mom and I opened up the two cards, and I asked her if she could read them to me. To my astonishment, even though our conversation remained gibberish, she could read many of the loving words. Encouragement began to seep into my veins, breathing life back into my heart. Hope of regaining some of my mom back made a resurgence—momentarily.

June 26

The joy of my mama's birthday came to a screeching halt with the early morning phone call from the hospital—the first of several. Mom had gotten out of her chair, stood up, and began to fall just before the nurses got to her. She was being rushed to radiology to determine the extent of her injury. It was later determined that her hip and leg were broken in several places, and the surgeon was being called in.

I arrived at Mama's bedside in the pre-op room shortly before surgery. Her brown eyes that could always see straight into my heart welcomed me. I fought back my own fear when, for the first time ever, she told me she was scared. No gibberish came from her lips. She was heavily sedated due to pain, but she was fully cognitive, and I understood every cherished word she spoke to me. I held her hand and kept my face close to hers. I stroked her hair and kissed her softly on the lips. I began to pray out loud as the staff compassionately looked on. I then began to pray the Lord's Prayer, as Mama and I had done every night for months. She prayed it with me, remembering nearly all of the words this time. She was fully my mama for what would be the last time, yet I embraced her as my innocent child. My tears were kept in check until they needed to escort her away. I told her how much I loved her, that everything would be okay, and promised I would be waiting for her.

As they wheeled her away, I looked at my watch. Church was starting in five minutes. Rather than pacing in the lonely waiting room, I ran to my car to go to church. I got back to the hospital just in time to talk with the doctor and spend the rest of the day with my precious mom.

June 27

After work, I was anxious to get back to the hospital to help Mom eat her dinner. She had already begun a resistance to eating and drinking, but I valiantly tried to sneak in as much nutrition as possible. I noticed that her breathing appeared to have become labored and wished somehow my sister could see what I saw. She is a registered nurse with a lot of experience in trauma, and I valued her opinion.

I leaned into Mama and told her how much I loved her. She returned a meek, "I love you too." Then I realized what I needed to do. I took a video clip of Mom on my phone, showing her breathing, and sent it to my sister. I also decided to record one more video clip. I told my mama I loved her, she turned her head toward me, and with her sparkling brown eyes looking deep into my soul, she said again, "Ohhh, I love you too." Hesitation nearly ruined the moment, but I felt encouragement from the God who loves me that it would be my last opportunity to record such a priceless moment. Millstone? What millstone? I traded in the millstone for a memory, a visual legacy of my mama's love, just like the video my dad bestowed upon me years earlier.

A short time later, a nurse came in to check on Mom. We were concerned about her urine output, and the nurse wanted to try to adjust the catheter. I instantly knew this would be a problem for Mom. I held her hand tightly and once again pressed in close to her beautiful face, which showed the paralysis of terror. The nurse adjusted Mom's gown, and Mom began to cry, screamed "No," and kept pulling her gown back down. She was reliving the time of her abuse as a child.

I told Mom, "It's okay, Mama. This is Cheryl, and I'm right here. These are nurses, and they're helping to make you feel better. It's okay, Mama. It's okay." My heart, soul, and spirit were sobbing with brokenness for the horror my dear mama had to relive. Yet I praised God that he chose me to regift his grace in lavish portions to the one who gave me life whom I loved more than my own life.

June 29

I spent over an hour and several terse phone calls to deny the hospital's desire to discharge my Mom. A transfusion replenished her with two units of blood, but she never walked a single step, refused to eat, couldn't breathe very well, and was at an incredibly high risk to fall again. Mama Bear came out again and would not be denied. The compromise was to return my mama to the psychiatric floor and her mainstay location in the day room.

When I arrived in the early evening to once again assist her in eating her dinner, she refused all food. She was physically uncomfortable and complained that her stomach hurt. But I knew she knew who I was, because her face lit up every time she would look at me. And when I asked her who I was, she proclaimed, "You're my daughter Cheryl."

But I knew this night was different. As I frequently did, I told her that when Jesus came for her, she could go with him. Her mournful, sunken eyes followed me wherever I walked, which was never more than a few steps away from her. The doctors ordered an EKG. I walked alongside mama's wheelchair as the nurse and I wheeled her back slowly to her room.

The EKG technician came with the portable cart. Mom graciously allowed her to wire her up and run the test, which was the first of many she would have in her final sixteen hours. I could tell by the forlorn look given to me by the technician that something was wrong. She quietly left the room, and my mama and I were given the gift of ten minutes alone after the technician left.

I gently caressed my mama's hands—worn from her many years of compassion shown to others. Yet at this moment, I was stymied to know how to comfort her like she comforted me through the nearly six decades of my life. Again I told her how much I loved her and that I would miss her every day after she went to heaven. I thanked her for being my best friend and for loving me deeply and for trusting me with her life. The floor nurse returned. My final intimate moment with my beloved mama was interrupted, and we brought Mom back to the day room.

Her blood oxygen level began to struggle, and her EKG showed something was wrong. The staff allowed me to stay well beyond visiting hours as they tried to assist Mom, telling her to take deeper breaths. I finally resolved myself to holding her hand and saying goodbye. I gave her gentle kisses on her furrowed brow and on her soft lips that spoke encouragement into my soul for decades. I told her for the very last time how much I loved her. She told me for the very last time how much she loved me.

I regretted leaving that night, but I didn't want to get in the staff's way. On the way home, I prayed fervently that God wouldn't allow her to suffer anymore. Mom said long ago that she anticipated she would pass away in the month of June, just like her mother and her brother. I boldly prayed, "Lord, it's almost the end of June. It's time, Lord. It's time."

And I did battle with myself. I regretted going home to sleep simply because I knew the following day was a heavy work day. I should've stayed. I should've remained her advocate. I should've kissed her one more time. My shame-filled battle was in blatant defiance of all the compassionate care and love I gave her through this journey through *it*.

My final night was spent in self-inflicted shame. Mom's final night was a series of more EKGs, CT scans, and lab work, and it led to the final curtain of blood clots and a heart attack that will separate us until eternity.

June 30

Even before I got out of bed, I pleaded with God. "Lord, it's the last day of June. This would really be a great day for Mom to go home." I thought about the extreme hardship my sweet mama was going through. As I prayed with my eyes closed, I saw the most vibrant image in my mind that I had ever seen. It was a beautiful photo of my mama. Then I began to hear her voice in my mind, more vibrant than any auditory recording I had ever heard. I was watching a high-definition movie of my mom—every image and every sound was in high resolution.

I was fully awake and fully amazed. And being fully prepared . . .

I arrived at the hospital, where I knew my beloved mama angel would be escorted over the threshold to heaven. I quickly parked the car and began running to the crosswalk that would take me to the emergency room entrance. From a distance, I saw Pastor Kevin and his wife, Nicole, running to the same crosswalk and hoped they were looking for me. Foolish doubter! Of course God sent them for me.

We barely said a word as we ran through the automatic doors into the emergency room reception. My heart raced; my words were few. Pastor Kevin boldly told the young woman at the desk why we were there. She quickly escorted us to the family conference room. My heart sank as I was told the doctor would come in to speak with me right away. I didn't allow my fear to compromise God's promise that I would be with Mom when her soul went to heaven.

I frantically begged my cell phone to connect with my husband's voice so I could tell him my mama was not okay. The doctor walked in, and we stood face to face in the faintly-lit room. During our two-minute conversation, a frenzied nurse entered the room twice, needing the doctor's immediate attention regarding my mom.

During those moments with the doctor, unbeknownst to me, Mom's heart beat for the very last time. The doctor asked me for a family directive. Through the torrents of my salty tears, I pleaded with him, "She's been through enough, and please, I beg you, please let her go." The room began to swirl around me as he left the room. My body felt lifeless as I realized the magnitude of my pronouncement.

Ninety seconds later, we were escorted in the direction of her emergency room suite. That's when the nurse first told me her heart had stopped beating. My feet refused to move just short of the entrance to her room, and I'm sure I turned pale. I told the young nurse, "Whoa, wait just a second. I've never been with someone like this before." Gratefully he knew what I meant, gave me a gentle smile, and said, "You'll be okay. We'll walk you through it together."

With God's preparation and great peace, I quickly entered the suite and made a beeline to my mom. In my haste, I never noticed the nurses pulling the lifesaving lines and tubes from her body. Her skin was jaundiced, but her soft face and courageous hands filled me with the presence of my mama. There was no more labored breathing, no more gibberish, and no more confusion. I held her hand tightly and kissed her tenderly on the lips that had spoken love into my soul for fifty-eight years. I looked upwards as my tear ducts finally unleashed the tsunami of tears I could no longer contain. Medical staff went in and out as I lamented, cried, and prayed— and praised. Pastor Kevin and Nicole joined with me in a festival of prayer, which culminated in praying the Lord's Prayer and telling Mom to be free to fly.

God's presence filled the room. At times, the suite seemed to spin as I tried to keep focused on this moment with the woman I loved with my whole heart for my whole life. While holding Mama's hand, I called Chuck and then each of my sons, and I asked Nicole for more tissues.

The coroner came in to introduce himself. I continued to hold my mom's hand as I turned to greet him and said, "Is it okay if I hate you?" I flashed a smile, and he graciously responded, "Most people feel that way too."

I turned my attention back to Mom. All of a sudden, Mom's index finger twitched. I wanted to scream, "She's alive!" But I was afraid they'd bring me up to the psychiatric floor. I stared into her face and quickly wrote off the twitch as something that happens right after death. That thought was quickly dismissed when a spark, like static electricity, passed from Mom's finger through mine, and I realized that her heart had stopped more than fifteen minutes earlier. And there were no wires connecting her to any machine.

I recalled my prayers to my heavenly Father, who prepared me in advance, to be with Mom when her spirit passed, and I was reminded of the power of grace and the realness of God and his presence. I believed my earnest prayers in the car were fulfilled. Her heart stopped immediately after I arrived in the emergency department, and her time of death was noted as three minutes after I first held her hand. He answered my prayer to be with her through the death of her body, and he answered my prayer to be with her during the release of her spirit. Perhaps the twitch was Mama reaching for Jesus, like she did many times during her final Sundays at church. Perhaps the surge was when her spirit first touched Jesus. Moments later, the room felt very empty, even though many people were still there. I silently praised my Creator for his faithfulness, and then methodically took care of business with the coroner, the funeral director who also buried my father, and the hospital staff.

After they all left, except for Kevin and Nicole, Kevin's cell phone rang—our senior pastor, Tad, was calling to pray with us. Since it was his birthday, we loudly serenaded him with "Happy Birthday." When we hung up, Kevin, Nicole, and I laughed over what the medical staff must have thought about hearing us sing "Happy Birthday"—loudly—in the emergency room—with Mom's body! With tears in our eyes, however, we recognized the appropriateness. Not only did we celebrate Pastor Tad's birthday, we celebrated my mama's new birth into her heavenly home!

Kevin and Nicole walked me to my car with Mom's possessions that were brought down to the emergency room from the psychiatric floor. My knees were shaking, and my heart was numb. After warm hugs, I told them I needed to go back up to the sixth floor to thank the nurses who treated my mom with such an abundance of love and compassion. I went back, alone, into the hospital through another entrance and walked down the corridor. As I approached the elevators, I looked down the even longer hallway past the elevators. I saw the funeral director escorting my mom's gurney out the back doors of the hospital. I wanted to run to catch them. *What for?* I didn't have an answer, so I paused instead to fend off more tears.

Three women were near the elevators and watched as sadness engulfed my countenance. They asked if I was okay. I explained that I just saw my mom down the small hallway, and that she had passed an hour earlier. The floodgates of tears opened again, and one of the women, all of whom were nurses, held me in her arms as I wept. She asked me where I was going, pushed the elevator button to the sixth floor, and escorted me upstairs. I never saw those three angels again, but I knew they were delicately positioned there by God just for me. Just like when God sent the angel with skin on when I contemplated the end of my life forty years earlier at the lake. I never saw her again either.

I visited with the nurses on the sixth floor, and we cried together. They truly loved my mom, despite her often-rugged demeanor. We realized that some of Mom's things were still there. We gathered up Mom's remaining possessions and lovingly bagged them up. After a series of more hugs and tears, I escorted myself through the security doors of the psychiatric unit for the final time.

The metallic, empty elevator took me to the ground floor, and I proceeded to walk through the seemingly empty corridor filled with the empty faces of lonely strangers, carrying in each hand a final bag of the tangible remnants of Mom's painful journey home. I exited through the emergency entrance I had frantically entered ninety minutes earlier, pausing long enough to wonder how many other families' lives were being changed at that moment in time, just like mine had been.

Despite standing on God's promises and equipped in his spiritual armor, my extreme sadness over never again hearing her voice, picking up the phone to call her, taking her to church, and seeing her eyes sparkle and her smile penetrate my heart made this the hardest journey of my life, except when I am reminded that God's grace carried me *through* it all. He touched me *in* it by teaching me virtues in my relationship with him and virtues in how to treat others.

During my season of grieving, my husband and I went to see the movie *Collateral Beauty*, starring Will Smith. Watching it offered me a valuable lesson. It's easy to see collateral damage when painful things happen. But it would be a shame to miss out on the surrounding collateral beauty. God allowed me to share in my mom's life and her passage back to undefeated innocence. I gained special, loving moments I would have missed if I hadn't been involved and if I hadn't taken up a proper vantage point to see them. I experienced God's grace and my mama's love—collateral beauty worth searching for.

I will forever rejoice that God selected me for this role of caregiver in both my parents' lives, particularly for my sweet mama. I intimately shared in her final three years of life, filling us both with hope, joy, peace, and love. The reality is that we intimately shared fifty-eight years of my life too. She was the life partner God gave me to be my angel on earth. And we loved each other like crazy.

Because I Caregave
I miss the softness of your hands, because I held them.
I miss the softness of your voice, because I listened.
I miss the softness of your lips, because I kissed them.
I miss the softness of your eyes, because I gazed into them.
I miss the softness of your heart, because I knew it.
I miss the softness of your soul, because I felt it.
I miss the softness of your tears, because I wiped them away.
I miss the softness of your smile, because we laughed.
I miss the softness of your skin, because I stroked your face.
I miss the softness of your hugs, because we shared them.
I miss the softness of your love, because I shared it.

Thank you for granting me the chance to share a fragment of my story with you. I wrote it with you in mind. If your stone is to be a caregiver, you are already equipped with a battle buddy who will never fail you. He won't ask you to do anything he doesn't first equip you to do.

Looking for undefeated innocence and grace? Keep looking in all the right places.

You might occasionally find it in a sock drawer.

We celebrated Mom's 80th birthday, and
she thanked us with a bow.

Resources

Organizations:

Alzheimer's Association
225 N. Michigan Avenue, Fl. 17, Chicago, IL 60601
800.272.3900
www.alz.org

Broyles Foundation
3810 N. Front Street, Fayetteville, AR 72703
479.313.5079
www.broylesfoundation.com
Publication: *Coach Broyles' Playbook for Alzheimer's Caregivers: A Practical Tips Guide*
Support groups, continuing education for medical professional, family counseling, transition assistance, phone counseling, and resource assistance

The Leeza Gibbons Memory Foundation
9903 Santa Monica Boulevard, Suite 180, Beverly Hills, CA 90212
888.655.3392
www.leezascareconnection.org

Home Instead Senior Care
13323 California Street, Omaha, NE 68154
888.484.5759 or 402.498.4466
www.homeinstead.com
www.homeinsteadfoundation.org
In-home care services and resource information

Amy's Place
14 Sloan Street, Roswell, GA 30075
470.349.8349
www.amysplace.net
Memory café and support groups

Hospice of the Ozarks
701 Burnett Drive, Mountain Home, AR 72653
800.771.9596 or 870.508.1771
www.hospiceoftheozarks.org
www.hospiceoftheozarks.org/caregivers.html: *Eleven Steps to Take When Caring for a Loved One*
Hospice services, grief support, and resource information for caregivers

Publications:

J. Frank Broyles, *Coach Broyles' Playbook for Alzheimer's Caregivers: A Practical Tips Guide* (Alzheimer's Assoc. 2006)

Nancy L. Mace et al., *The 36-Hour Day: A Family Guide to Caring for People with Alzheimer Disease, Other Dementias, and Memory Loss*, Sixth Edition (Johns Hopkins University Press 2017)

Additional Websites:

www.regiftedgrace.org
Regifted Grace Ministry LLC, *Regifted Grace: Experiencing and Sharing the Authority of God's Grace in Caregiving*
Resource information, book orders, and blog

www.spiritualgiftstest.com
Jeff Carver, *Spiritual Gifts Test*
Online test to discover your spiritual gifts

www.facebook.com
Numerous online dementia, caregiving, and grief support groups, including: *Alzheimers and Dementia Caregivers Support* and *Dementia Caregivers Support Group*

Endnotes

1 Alzheimer's Association, "2016 Alzheimer's Disease Facts and Figures" (2016), www.alz.org/facts.
2 Romans 8:28.
3 Romans 8:39.
4 John 15:26.
5 Isaiah 40:29.
6 Psalm 8:1–2.
7 Ephesians 1:14.
8 1 Corinthians 13:4–8a, 13.
9 Genesis 1:27.
10 John 3:16.
11 John 11:35.
12 Luke 18:42.
13 Romans 5:8; John 15:13; Revelation 1:5.
14 Galatians 2:20.
15 Hebrews 13:5.
16 Ephesians 3:17–19.
17 1 Thessalonians 1:10.
18 1 Timothy 1:12.
19 Romans 8:35, 38–39.
20 1 Peter 1:22.
21 Adapted from Psalm 107.
22 John 16:20, 22.
23 John 11:4.
24 John 11:32.
25 Elisabeth Kübler-Ross, MD, and David Kessler, *On Grief & Grieving: Finding the Meaning of Grief Through the Five Stages of Loss* (New York: Scribner 2014).

26 2 Corinthians 1:3–4)

27 Philippians 4:11–13.

28 1 Thessalonians 1:6.

29 Adapted from Psalm 23.

30 Isaiah 6:8.

31 Numbers 12:3.

32 Ephesians 6:12.

33 Psalm 37:11.

34 C. Ballard et al., "Anxiety, Depression and Psychosis in Vascular Dementia: Prevalence and Associations," *Journal of Affective Disorders* 59, no. 2 (August 2000): 97–106.

35 Adapted from Psalm 122:6–9.

36 Romans 3:22–24.

37 Romans 3:25–26.

38 Jeremiah 29:11.

39 Romans 5:3–4 (Scripture taken from *The Message*. Copyright © 1993, 1994, 1995, 1996, 2000, 2001, 2002. Used by permission of NavPress Publishing Group).

40 Romans 5:1–2 (Scripture taken from *The Message*. Copyright © 1993, 1994, 1995, 1996, 2000, 2001, 2002. Used by permission of NavPress Publishing Group).

41 Adapted from Psalm 145.

42 Ephesians 2:4–5.

43 Romans 8:31–39.

44 2 Corinthians 4:17.

45 Acts 9:17.

46 Nehemiah 9:31.

47 James 2:13.

48 John 14:1 (Scripture taken from the New Century Version®. Copyright © 2005 by Thomas Nelson. Used by permission. All rights reserved).

49 Colossians 3:12–14 (Scripture taken from *The Message*. Copyright © 1993, 1994, 1995, 1996, 2000, 2001, 2002. Used by permission of NavPress Publishing Group).

50 Psalm 31:9.

51 Psalm 6:2.

52 Psalm 40:11.

53 Psalm 57:1.

54 See www.koreanwarvetsmemorial.org for more information.

55 Romans 12:1–2.

56 Maria C. Norton PhD, et al., "Greater Risk of Dementia When Spouse Has Dementia? The Cache County Study," *Journal of the American Geriatrics Society* 58, no. 5 (May 2010): 895-900.

57 Edmarie Guzman-Velez et al., "Feelings Without Memory in Alzheimer Disease," *Cognitive and Behavioral Neurology* 27, no. 3 (2014): 117-129.

58 Ibid.

59 John Riehl, "Alzheimer's Patients Can Still Feel the Emotion Long After the Memories Have Vanished" (September 24, 2014), http://now.uiowa.edu/2014/09/alzheimers-patients-can-still-feel-emotion-long-after-memories-have-vanished.

60 Marc Lewis, *The Biology of Desire: Why Addiction is Not a Disease* (New York: PublicAffairs, 2015), 8.

61 Adapted from Psalm 31.

62 Siobhan T. O'Dwyer et al., "Suicidal Ideation in Family Carers of People with Dementia: A Pilot Study," *International Journal of Geriatric Psychiatry* 28, no. 1 (November 2013): 1182-1188.

63 Brian Draper, "Early Dementia Diagnosis and the Risk of Suicide and Euthanasia," *Alzheimer's & Dementia* 6, no. 1 (January 2010): 75-82; Lisa S. Seyfried et al., "Predictors of Suicide in Patients with Dementia," *Alzheimer's & Dementia* 7, no. 6 (November 2011): 576-573.

64 Centers for Disease Control and Prevention, "Suicide Facts at a Glance" (2015), www.cdc.gov/violenceprevention/pdf/suicide-datasheet-a.pdf.

65 Philippians 4:6-7 (Scripture taken from *The Message*. Copyright © 1993, 1994, 1995, 1996, 2000, 2001, 2002. Used by permission of NavPress Publishing Group).

66 James 4:8a, 10.

67 Tracy Kemble, Right Living Program, "Alone But Not Lonely (Healing from Abandonment and Rejection)," www.winfoundationinternational.org/alone.html.

68 See Daniel 3.

69 John 14:18 (The Living Bible copyright © 1971 by Tyndale House Foundation. Used by permission of Tyndale House Publishers Inc., Carol Stream, Illinois 60188. All rights reserved. The Living Bible, TLB, and the The Living Bible logo are registered trademarks of Tyndale House Publishers).

70 Philippians 1:18-20.

71 Philippians 2:14-15 (The Living Bible copyright © 1971 by Tyndale House Foundation. Used by permission of Tyndale House Publishers Inc., Carol Stream, Illinois 60188. All rights reserved. The Living Bible,

TLB, and the The Living Bible logo are registered trademarks of Tyndale House Publishers).

72 Romans 8:15–16 (The Living Bible copyright © 1971 by Tyndale House Foundation. Used by permission of Tyndale House Publishers Inc., Carol Stream, Illinois 60188. All rights reserved. The Living Bible, TLB, and the The Living Bible logo are registered trademarks of Tyndale House Publishers).

73 *Great Is Thy Faithfulness* by Thomas O. Chisholm © 1923, ren. 1951 Hope Publishing Company, Carol Stream, IL 60188, www.hopepublishing. com. All rights reserved. Used by permission.

74 Daniel 6:16 (The Living Bible copyright © 1971 by Tyndale House Foundation. Used by permission of Tyndale House Publishers Inc., Carol Stream, Illinois 60188. All rights reserved. The Living Bible, TLB, and the The Living Bible logo are registered trademarks of Tyndale House Publishers).

75 Daniel 6:25–27 (The Living Bible copyright © 1971 by Tyndale House Foundation. Used by permission of Tyndale House Publishers Inc., Carol Stream, Illinois 60188. All rights reserved. The Living Bible, TLB, and the The Living Bible logo are registered trademarks of Tyndale House Publishers).

76 Adapted from Psalm 57.

77 Isaiah 43:2 (The Living Bible copyright © 1971 by Tyndale House Foundation. Used by permission of Tyndale House Publishers Inc., Carol Stream, Illinois 60188. All rights reserved. The Living Bible, TLB, and the The Living Bible logo are registered trademarks of Tyndale House Publishers).

78 Ephesians 6:11–13.

79 Romans 8:26.

80 2 Corinthians 4:8–9 (The Living Bible copyright © 1971 by Tyndale House Foundation. Used by permission of Tyndale House Publishers Inc., Carol Stream, Illinois 60188. All rights reserved. The Living Bible, TLB, and the The Living Bible logo are registered trademarks of Tyndale House Publishers).

81 John 8:12.

82 Matthew 11:28–29.

83 Ephesians 1:7–9, 17.

84 Matthew 4:1-11.

85 Adapted from Psalm 18.

86 National Alliance for Caregiving and AARP, funded by MetLife Foundation, "Caregiving in the U.S. 2009," (November 2009), http://www.caregiving.org/data/Caregiving_in_the_US_2009_full_report.pdf.

87 MetLife Mature Market Institute, National Alliance for Caregiving, "The MetLife Caregiving Cost Study: Productivity Losses to U.S. Business" (July 2006), http://www.caregiving.org/data/Caregiver%20Cost%20Study.pdf.

88 MetLife Mature Market Institute, National Alliance for Caregiving, and The National Center on Women and Aging, "The MetLife Juggling Act Study: Balancing Caregiving with Work and the Costs Involved" (November 1999), http://www.caregiving.org/data/jugglingstudy.pdf.

89 Reported by The Women's Institute for a Secure Retirement, "The Effects of Caregiving" (2012), https://www.wiserwomen.org/images/imagefiles/The%20Effects%20of%20Caregiving.pdf.

90 Alzheimer's Association, "Take Care of Yourself: How to Recognize and Manage Caregiver Stress" (2015), https://www.alz.org/national/documents/brochure_caregiverstress.pdf.

91 SixWise.com, Epiphanies for Your Empowerment, "The Top Six Stressor Areas in your Life: How to Recognize & Handle the Stress," http://www.sixwise.com/newsletters/05/05/17/the-top-six-stressor-areas-in-life-how-to-recognize-amp-handle-the-stress.htm.

92 Caring.com, "Marriage Stress Survey," conducted January 8-15, 2009. Survey results and demographics located at https://www.caring.com/articles/love-and-marriage-and-caregiving.

93 1 Peter 3:14–18 (Scripture taken from *The Message.* Copyright © 1993, 1994, 1995, 1996, 2000, 2001, 2002. Used by permission of NavPress Publishing Group).

94 II Timothy 3:12.

95 John 15:18–19 or 2 Corinthians 12:10.

96 Luke 8:26–39.

97 1 John 4:18 (Scripture taken from *The Message.* Copyright © 1993, 1994, 1995, 1996, 2000, 2001, 2002. Used by permission of NavPress Publishing Group).

98 Matthew 14:22–33.

99 Joshua 24:15.

9 781512 778984